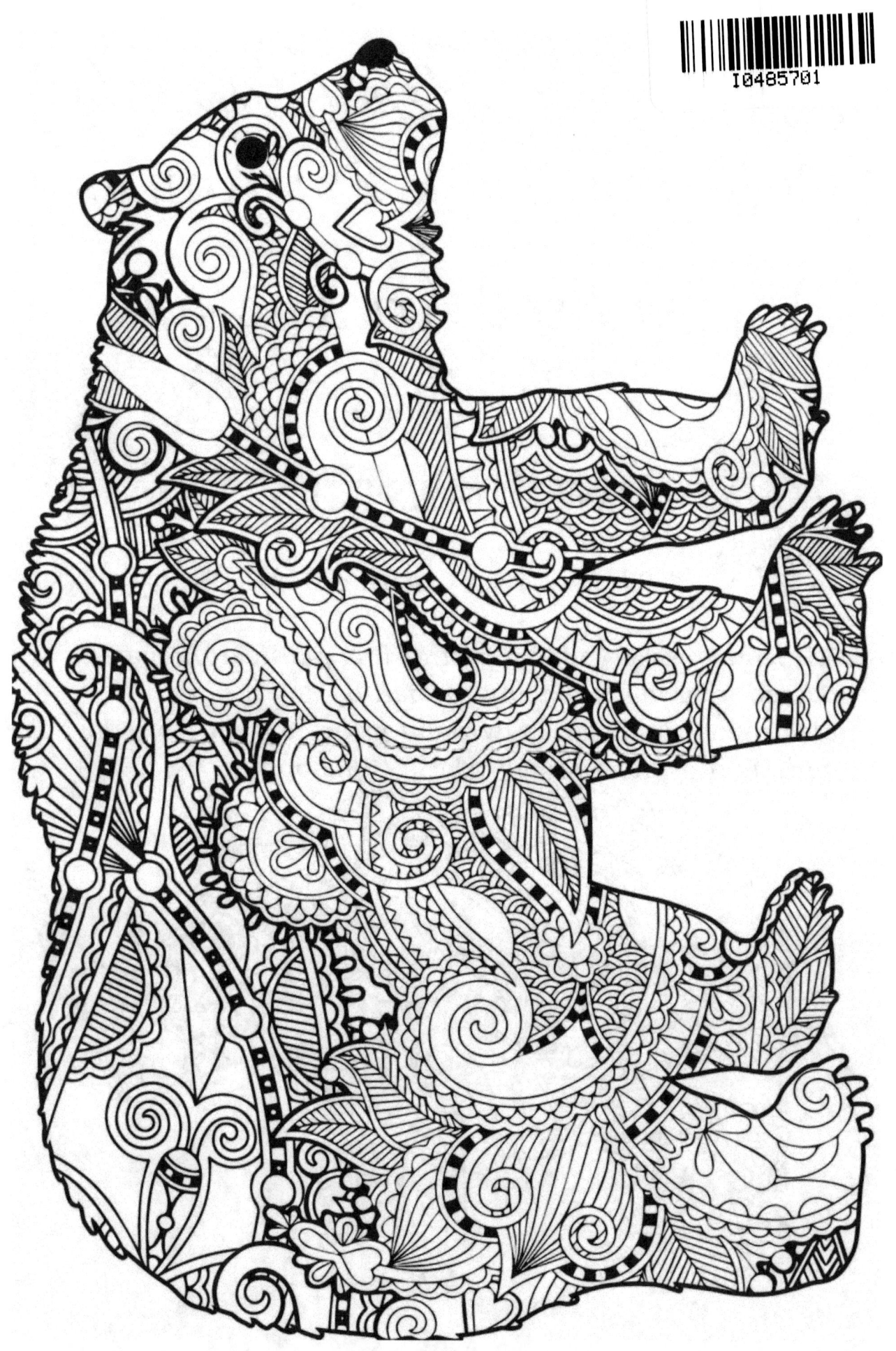

Intricate Zen Animals
Coloring Book For Adults

Stress Free Art Therapy
Volume 5

OWEN MASTERS

© 2015 by Avon Coloring Books

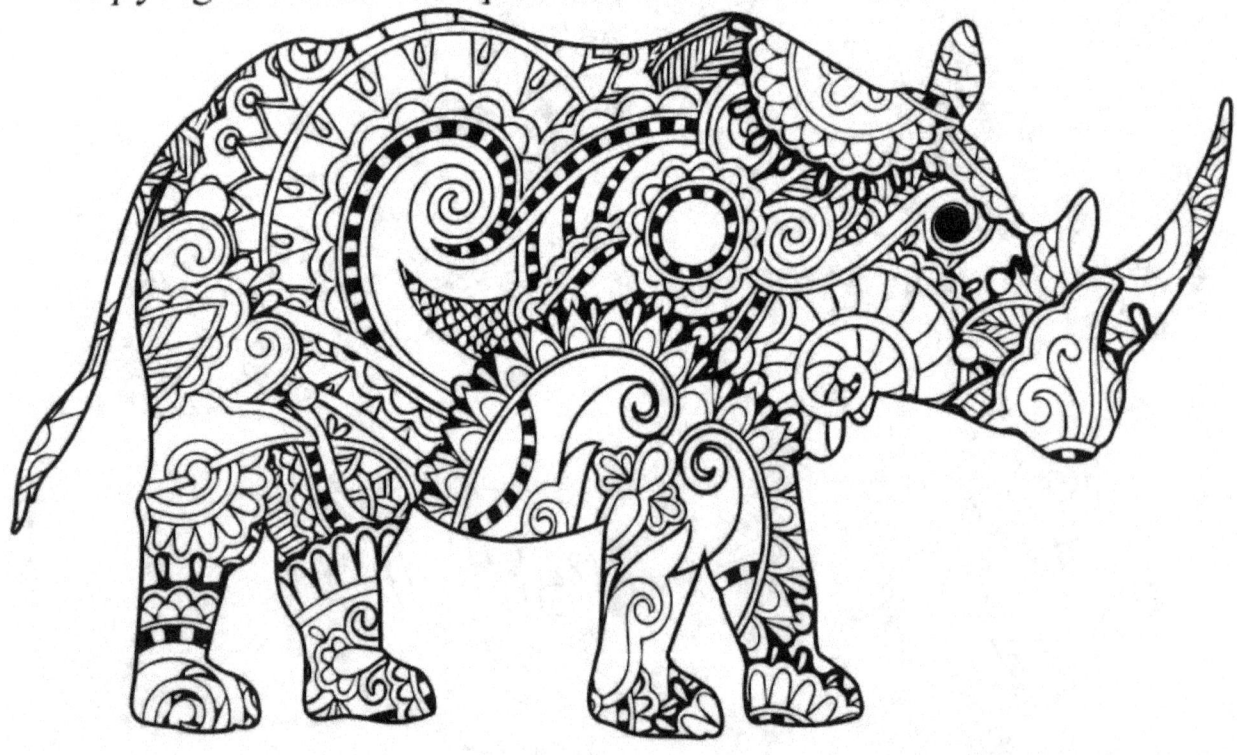

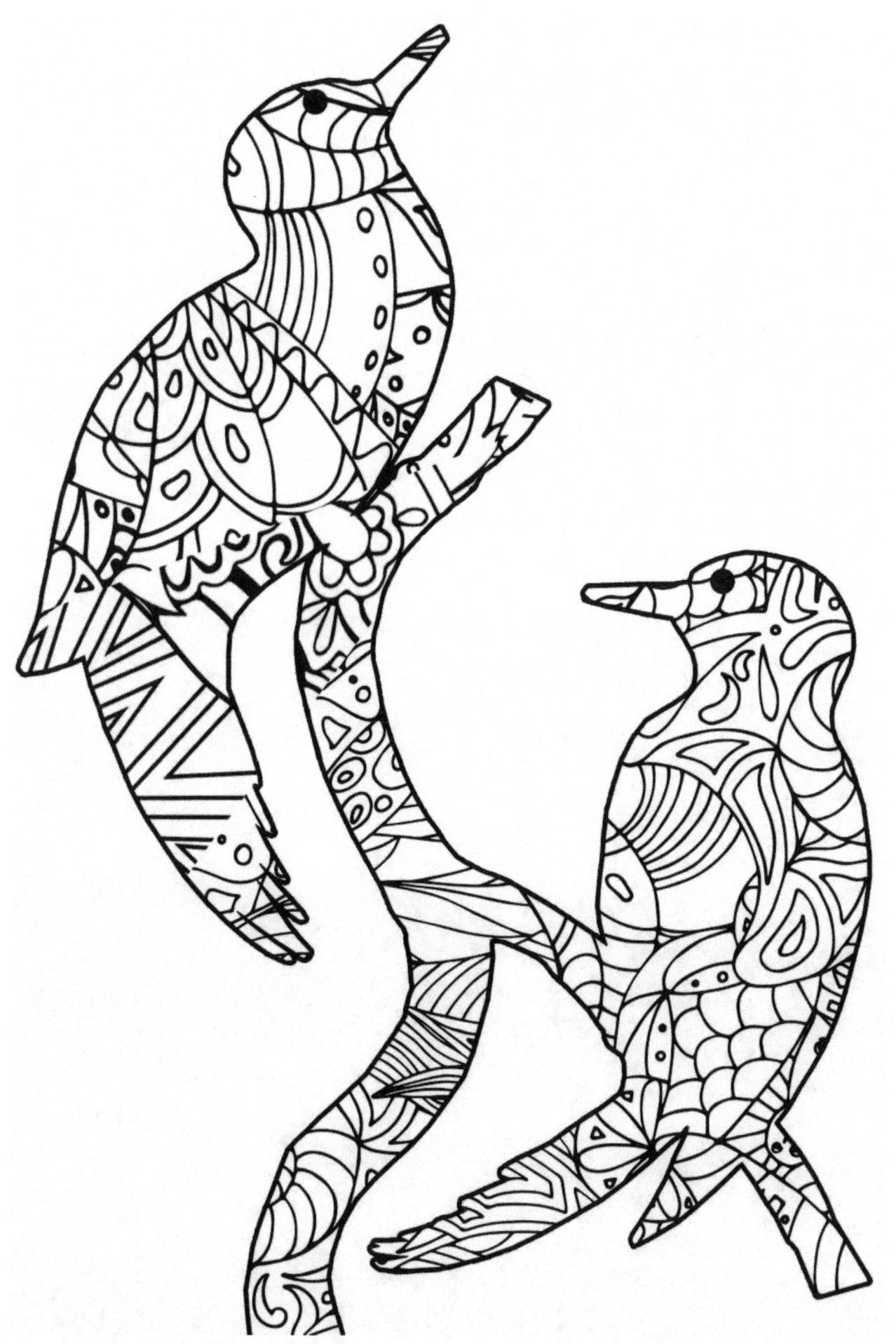

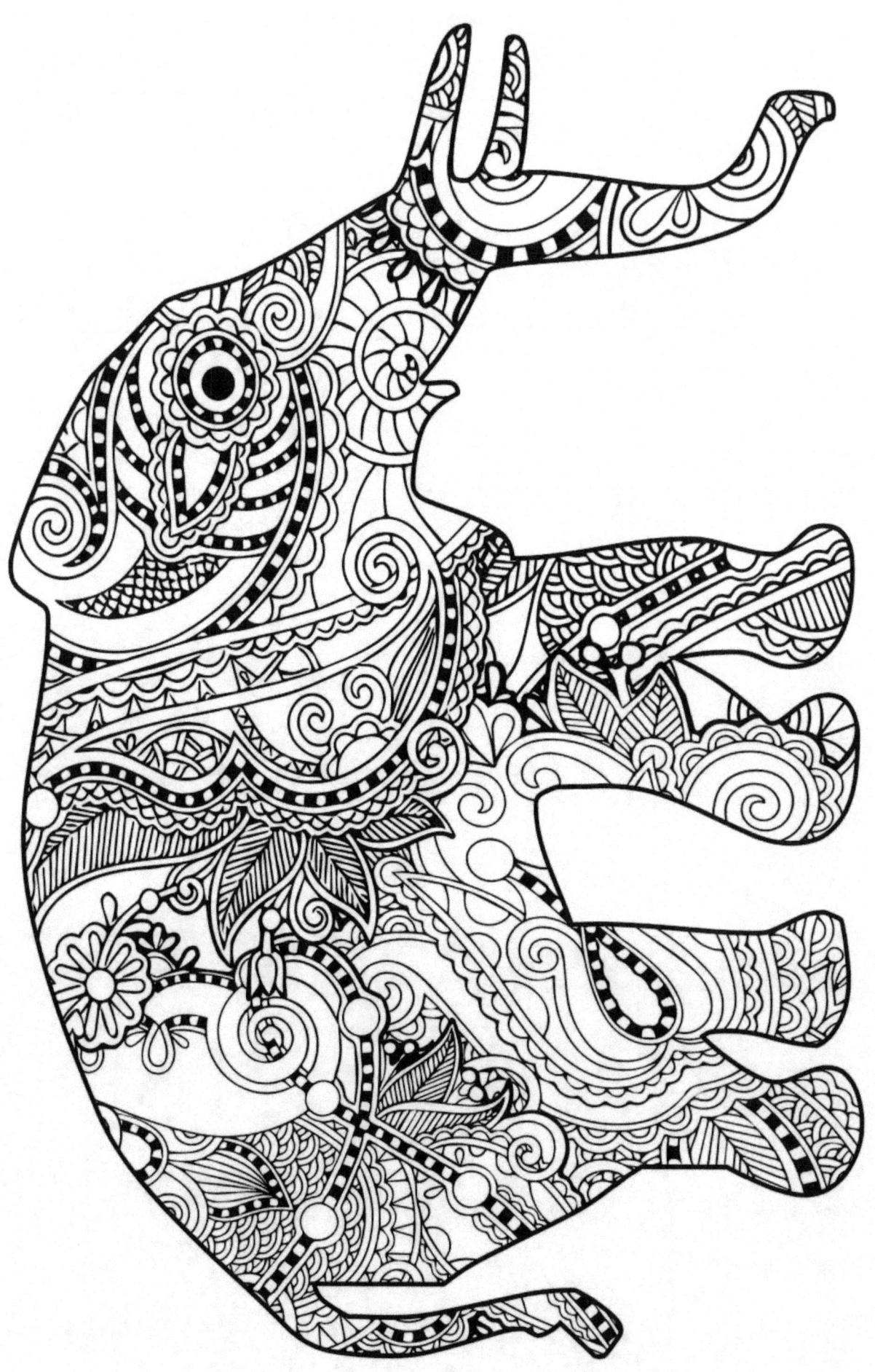

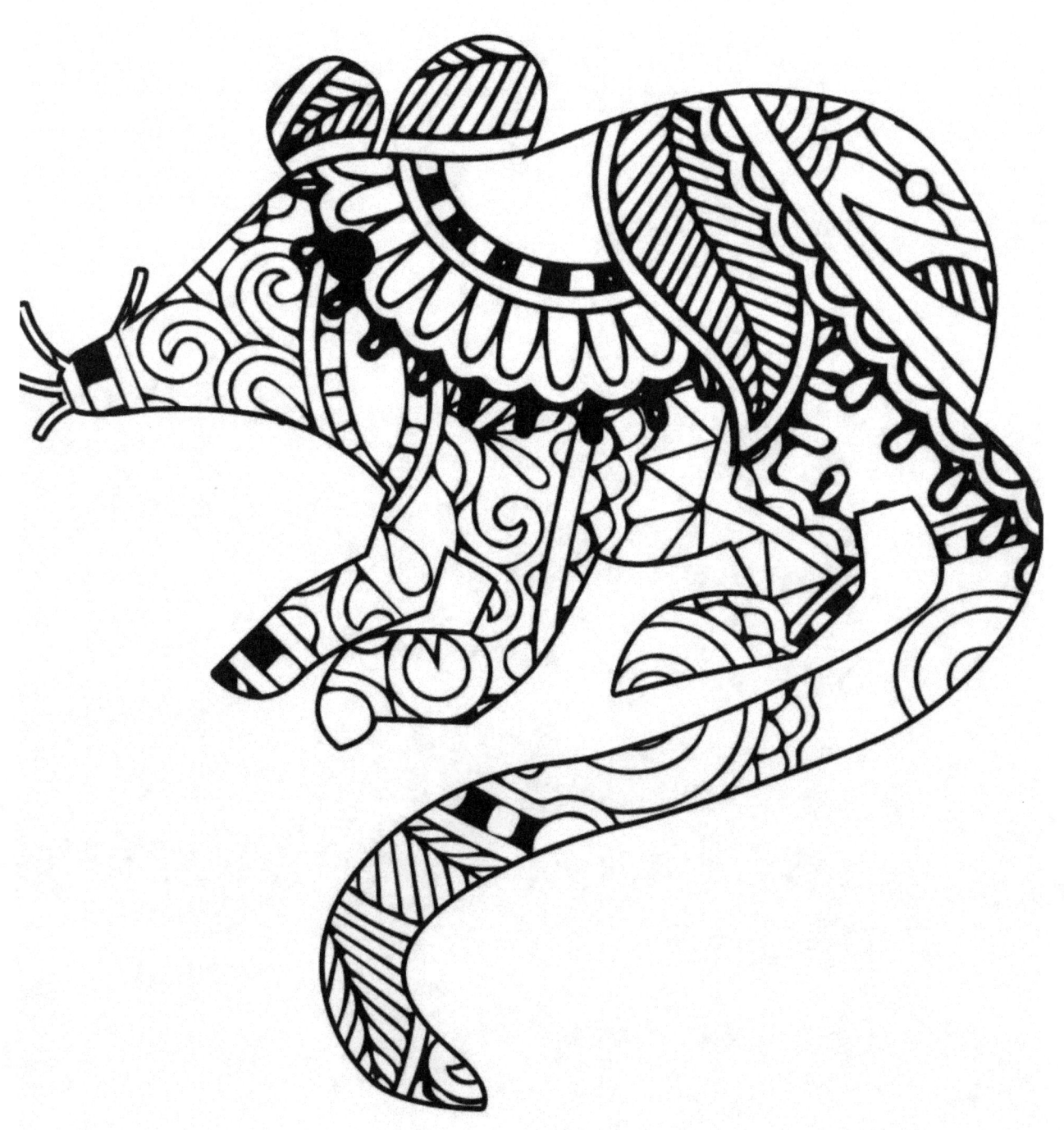

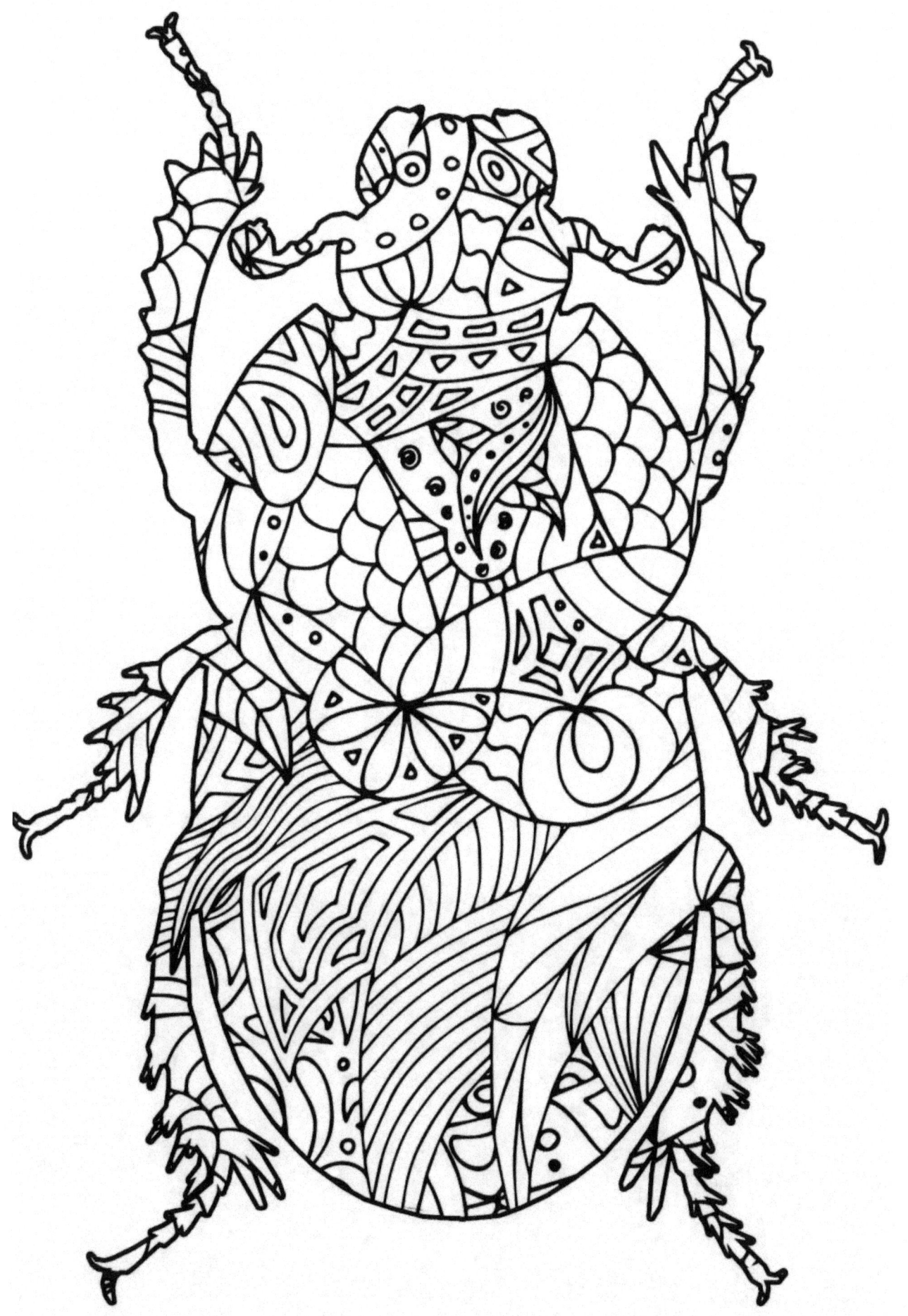

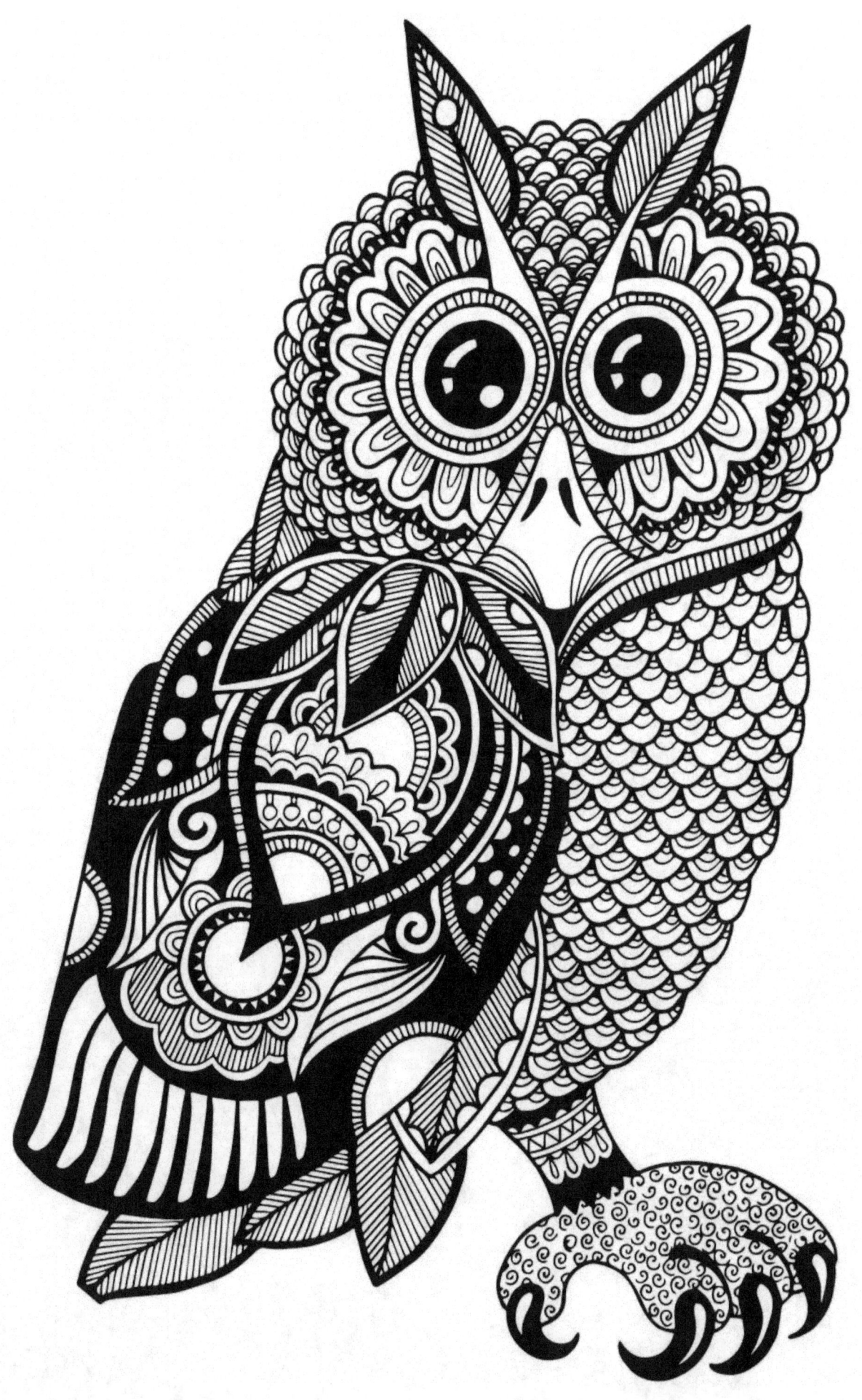

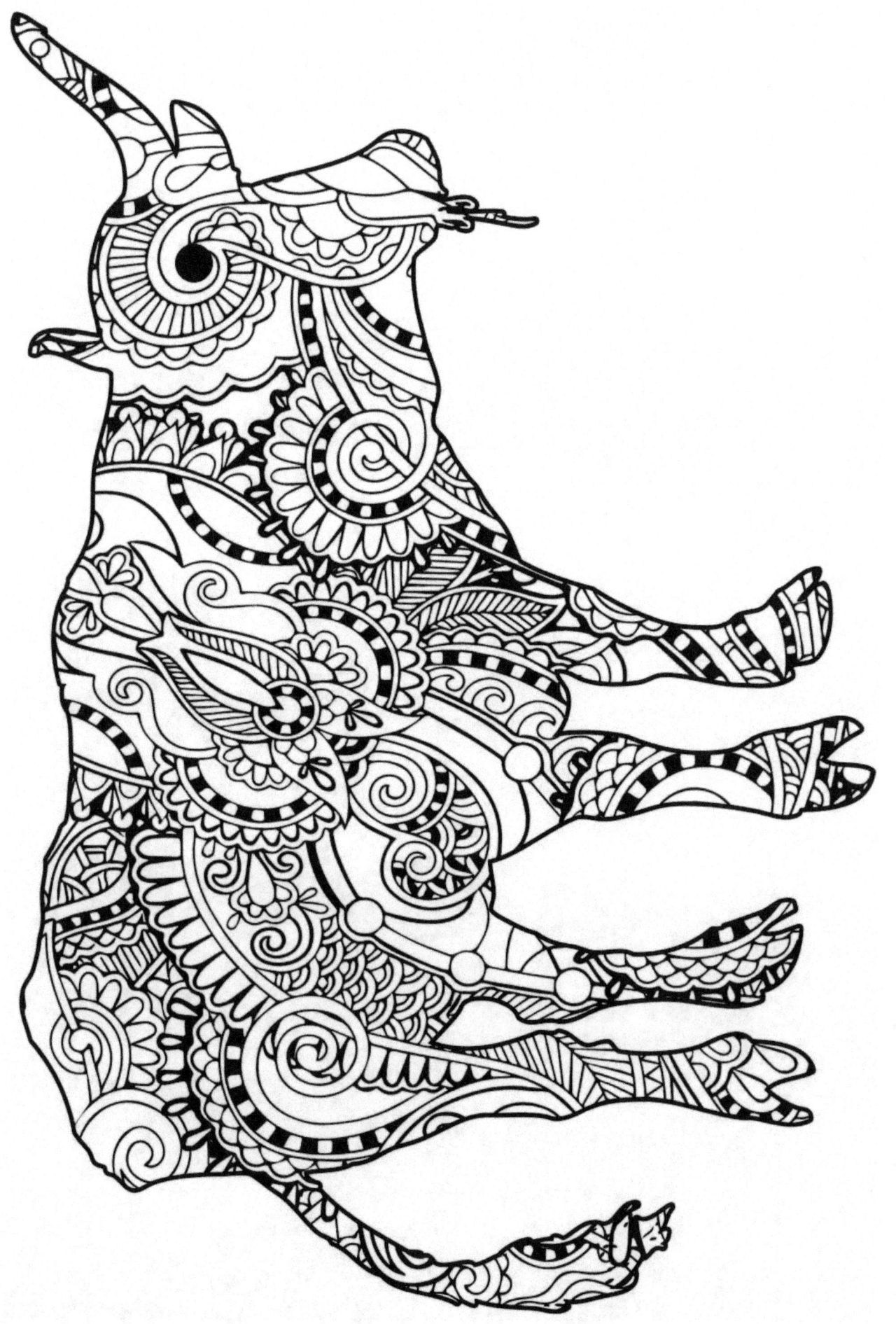

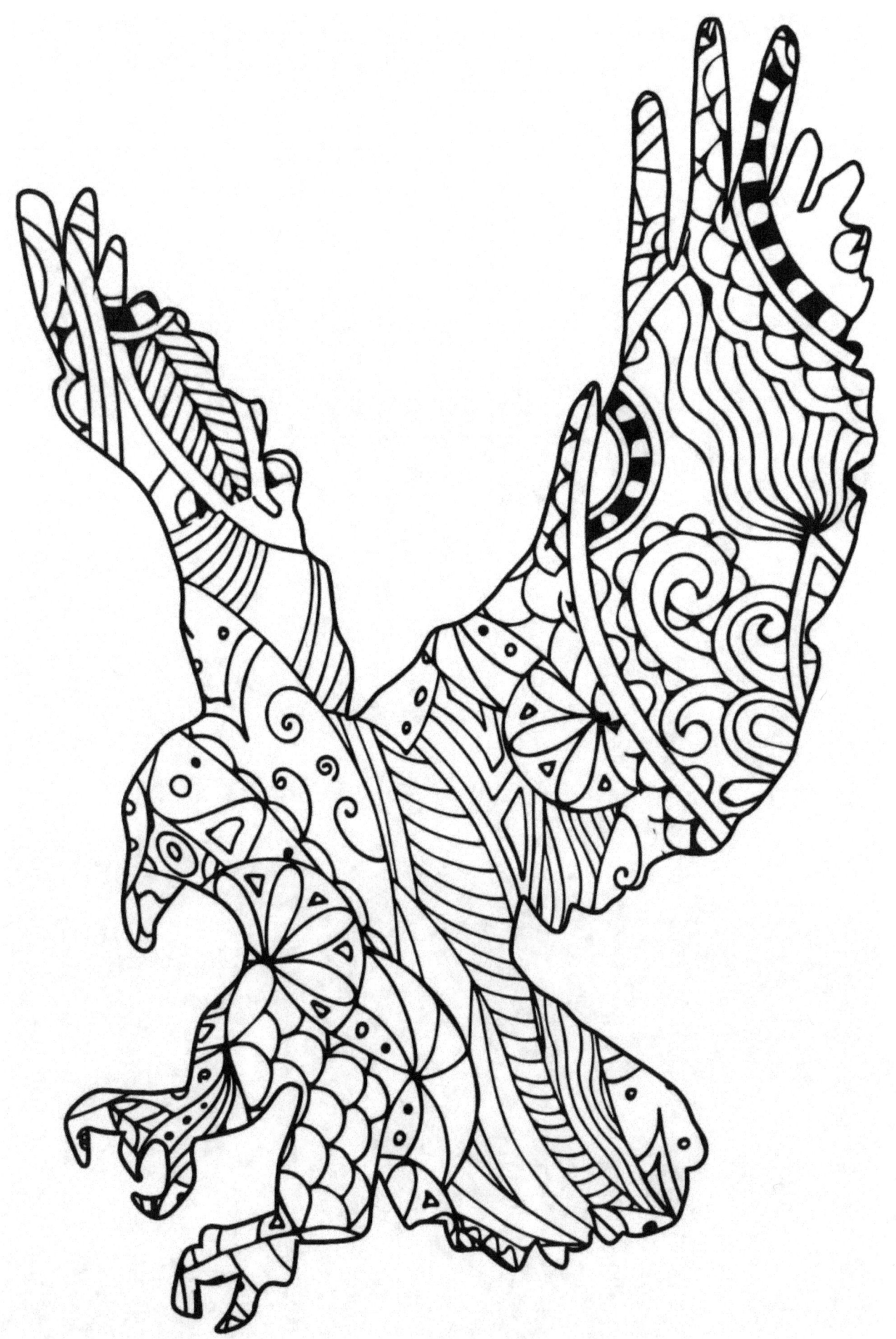

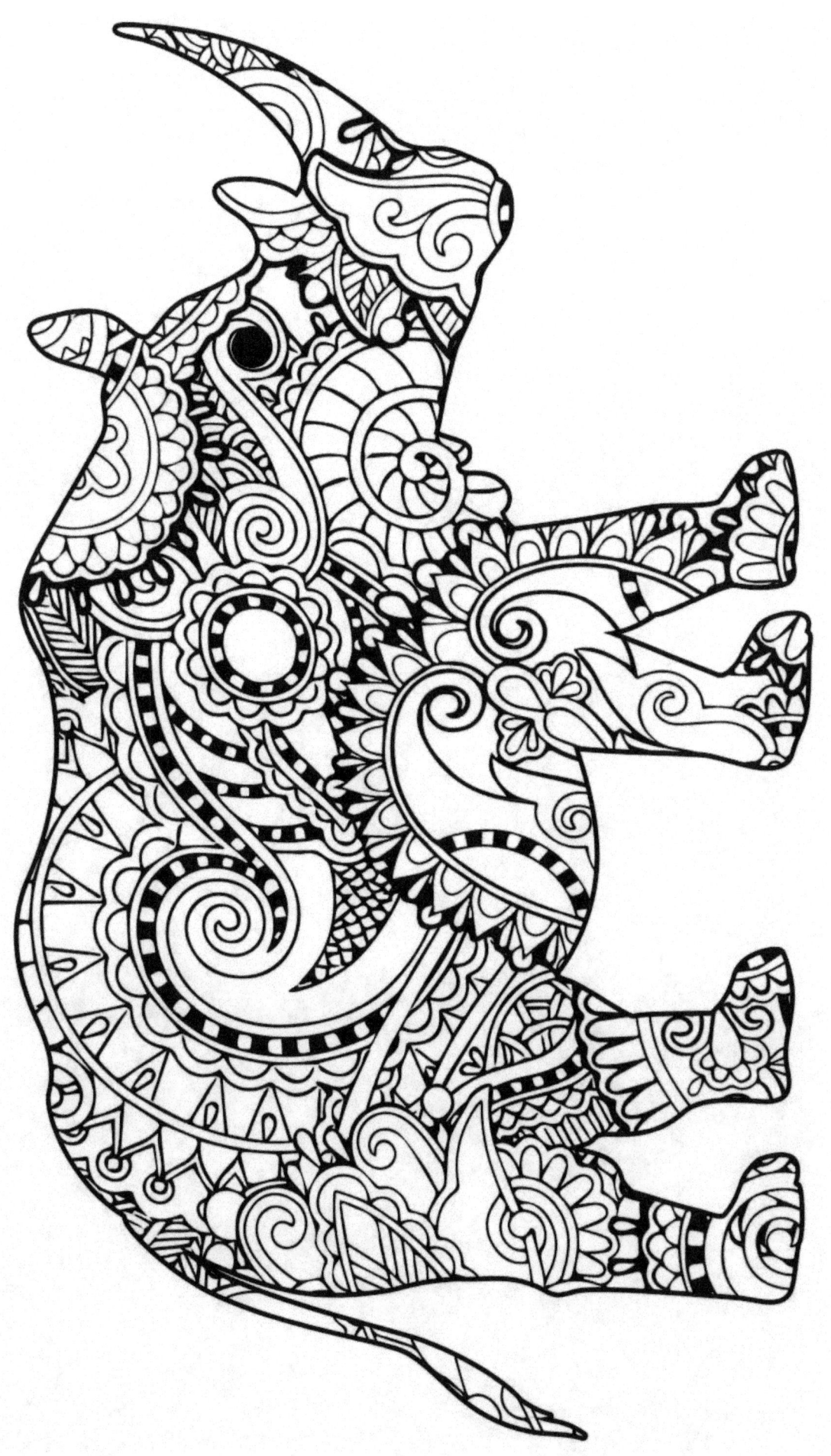

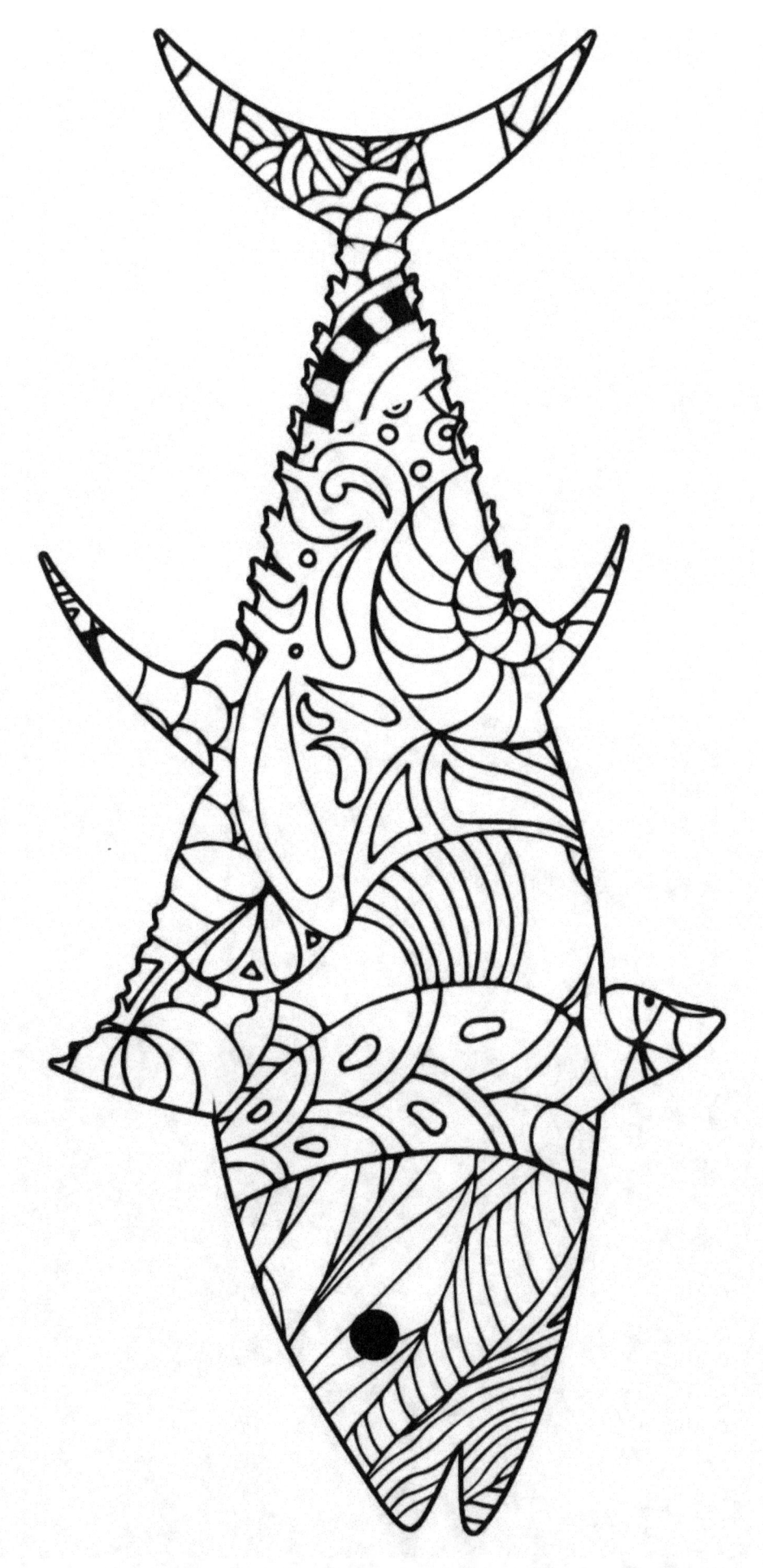

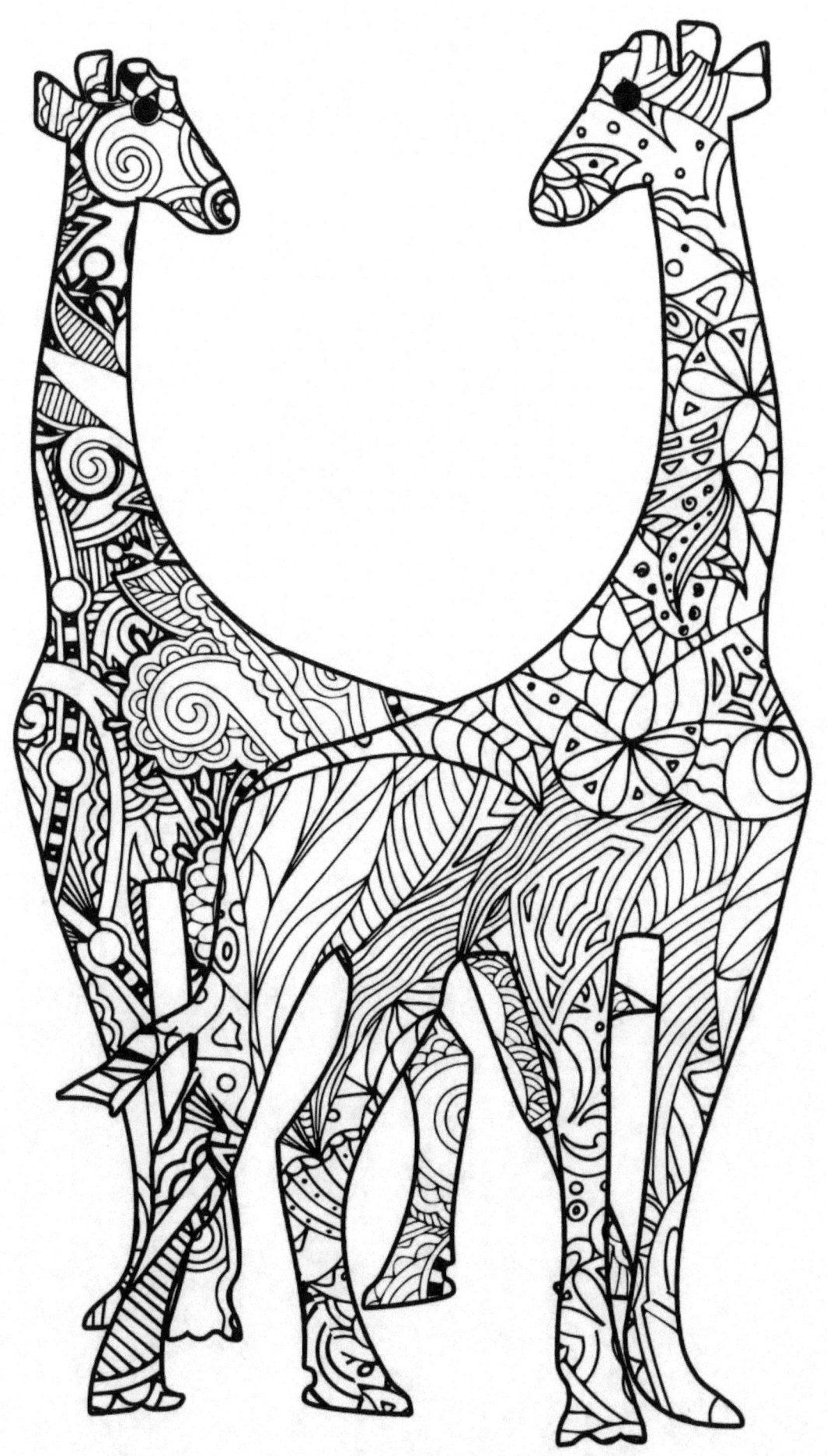

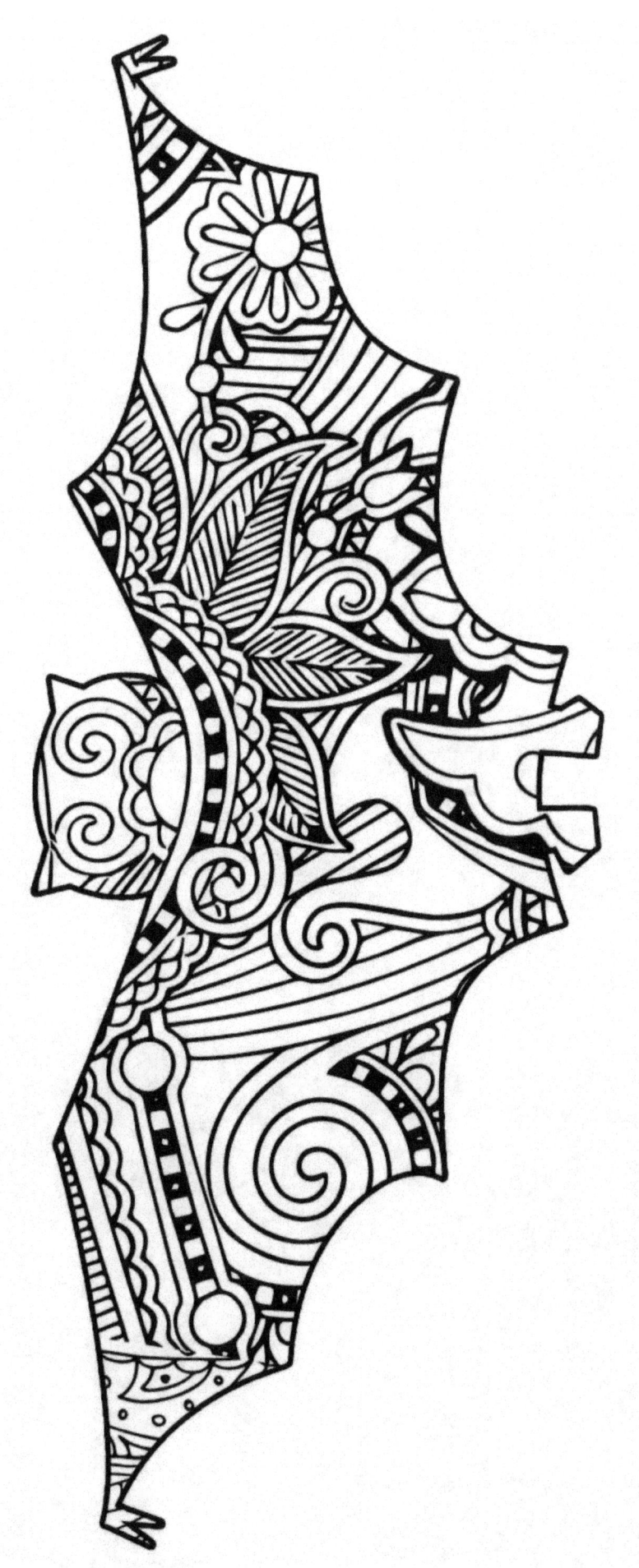

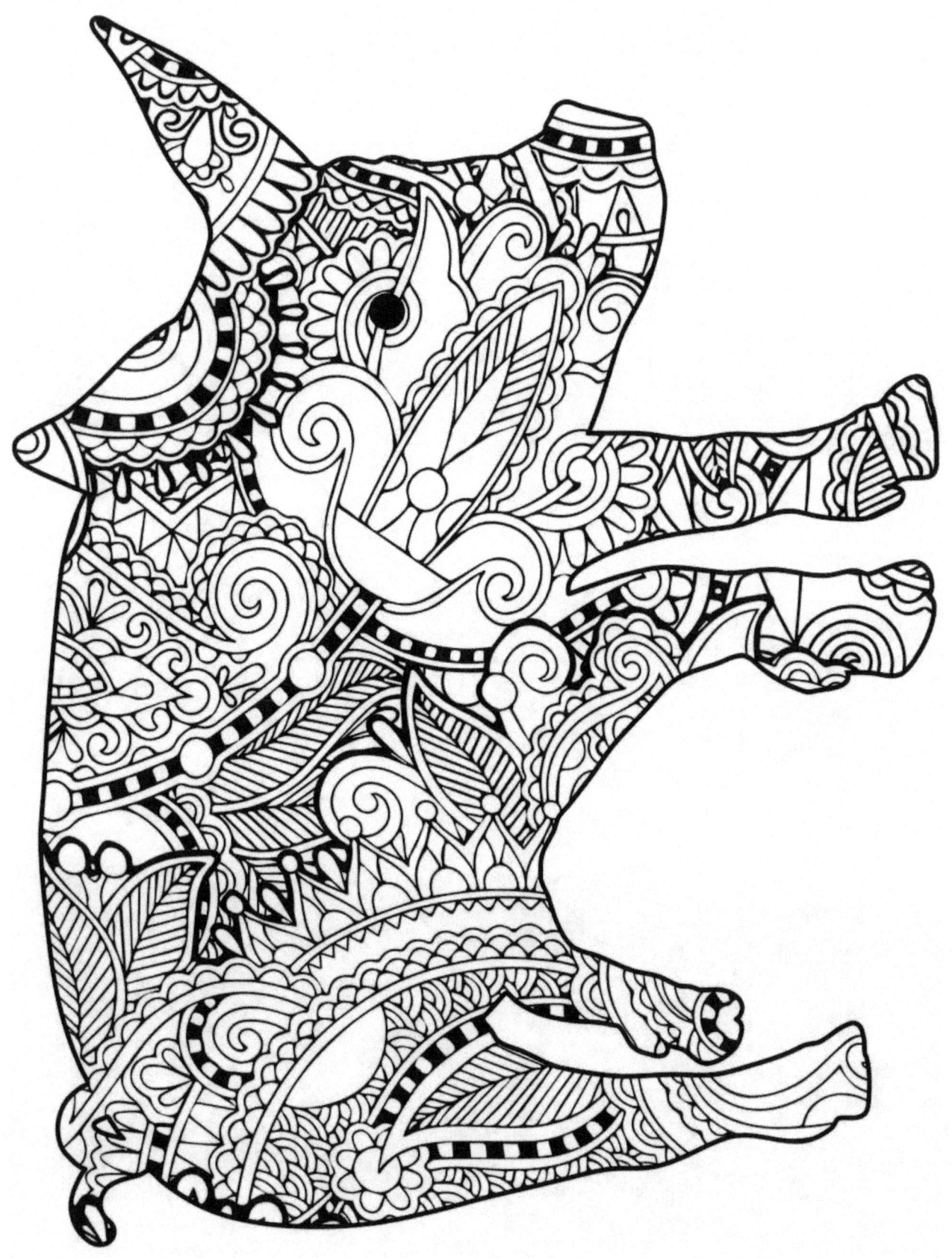

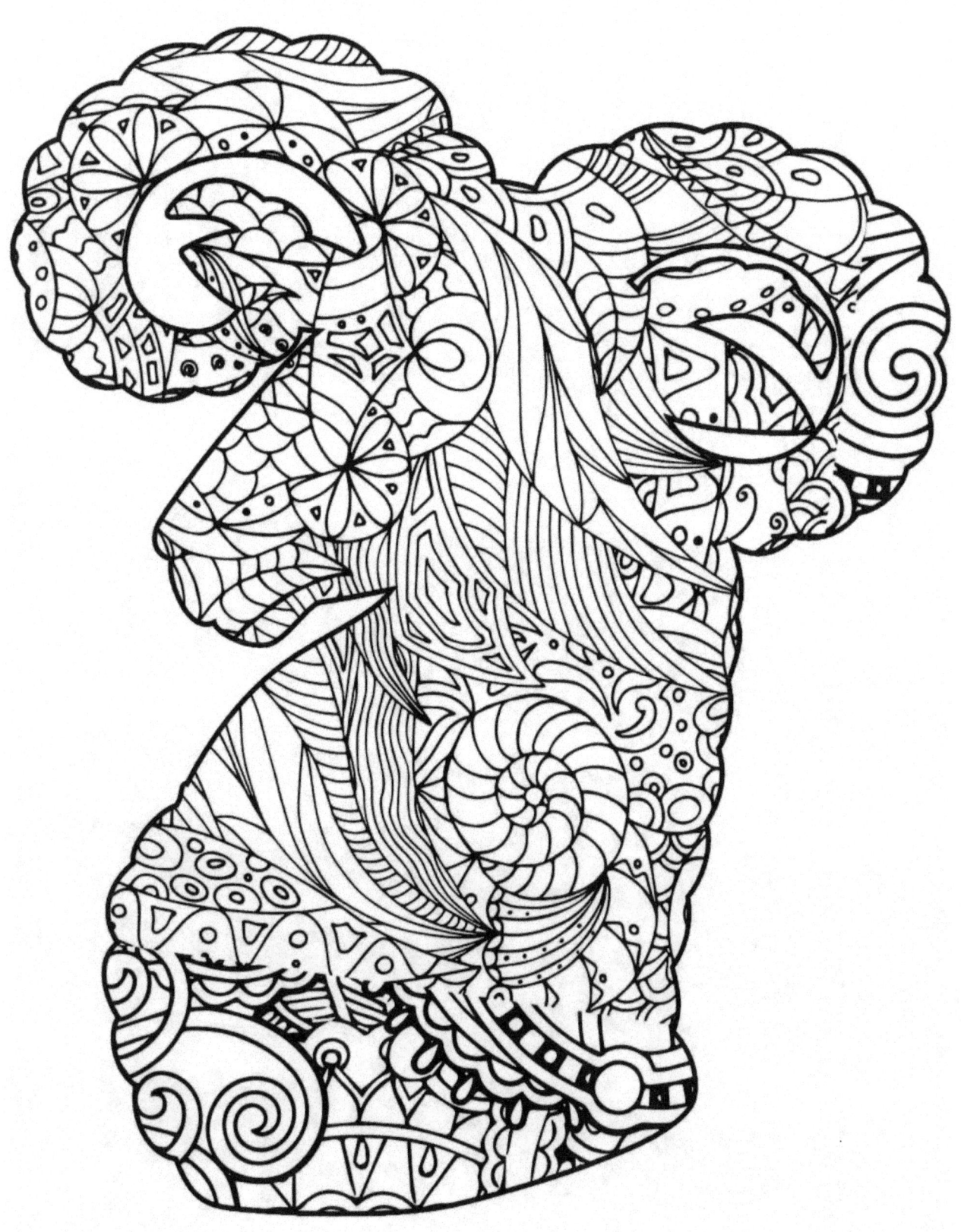

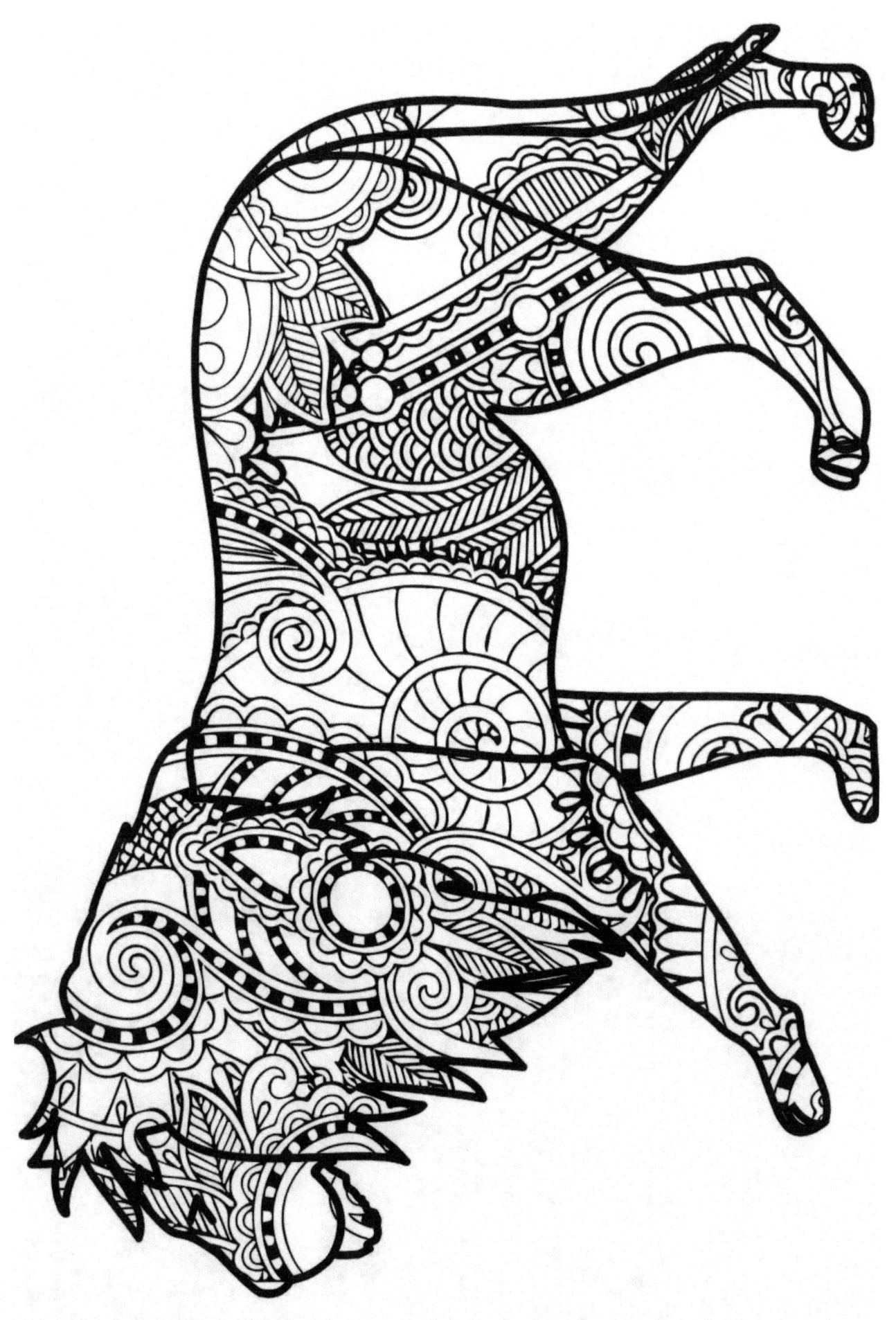

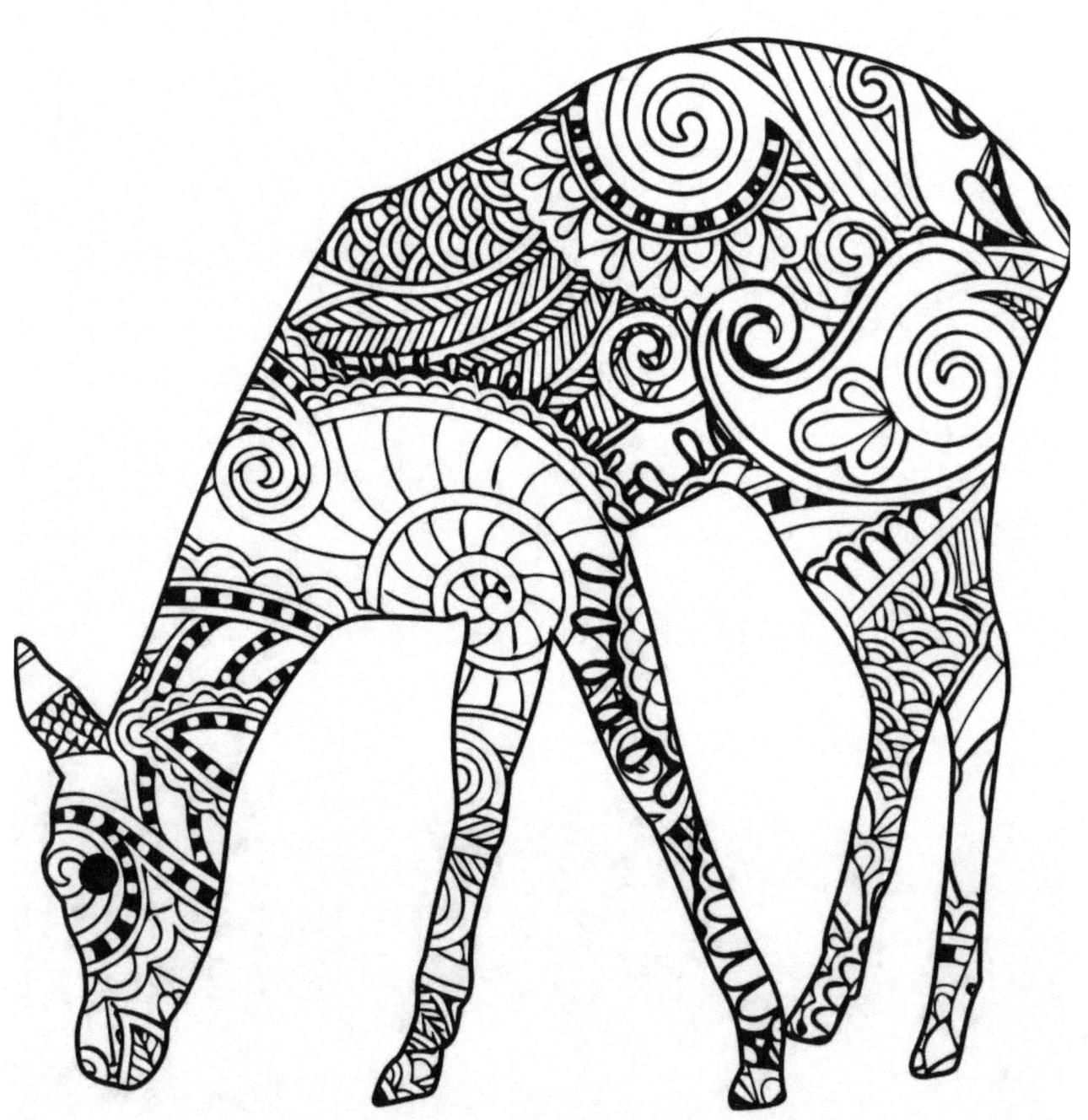

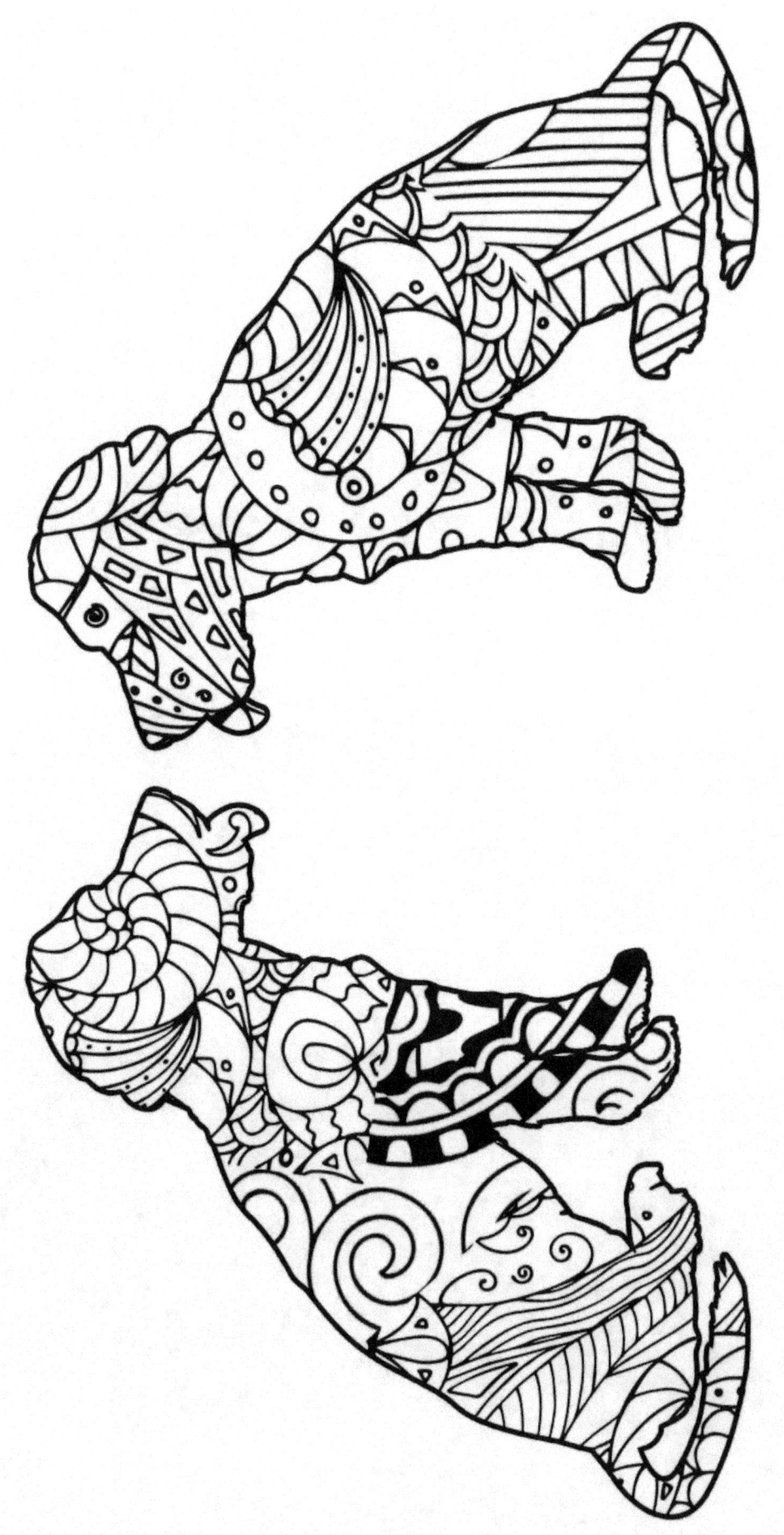

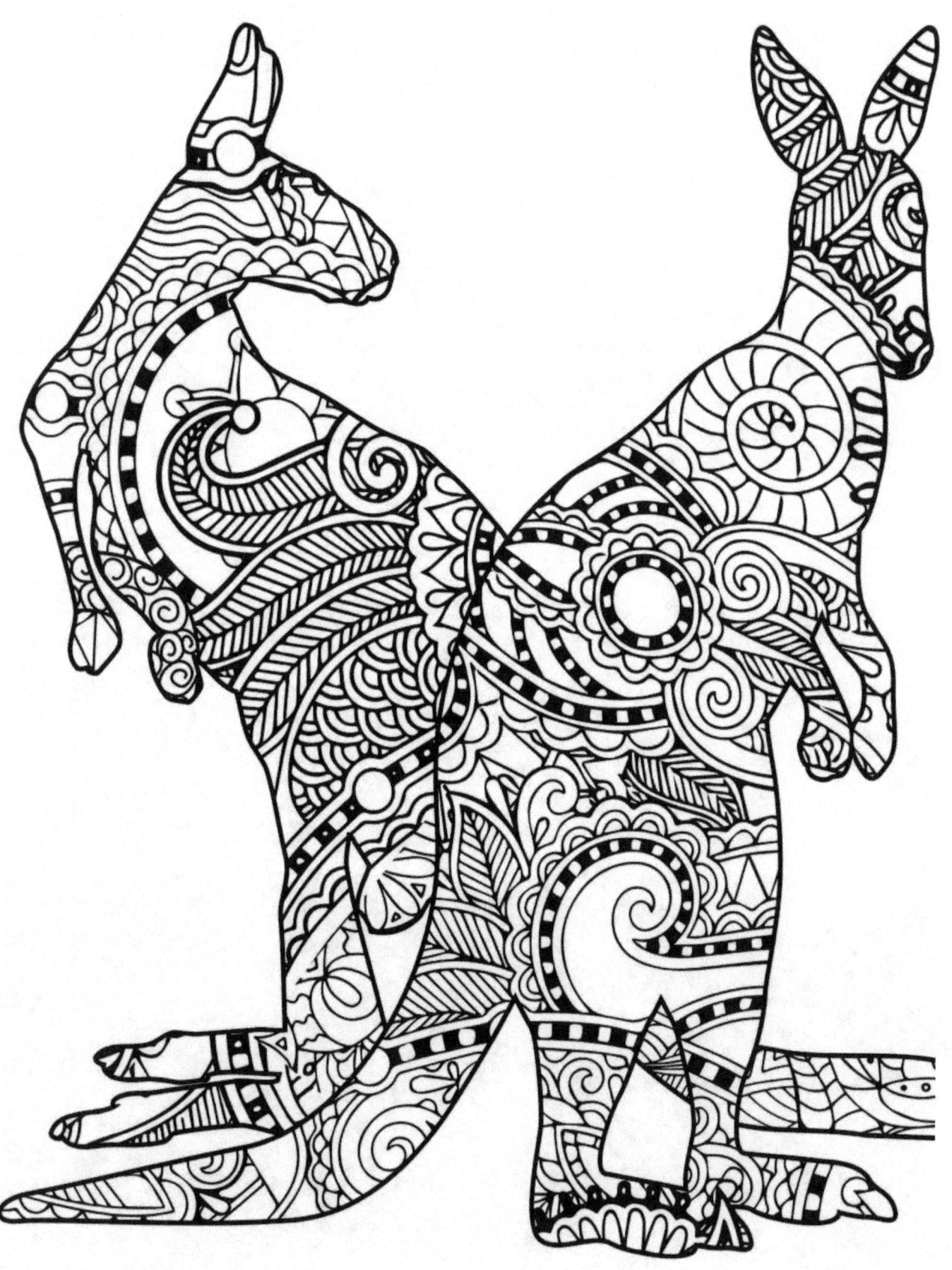

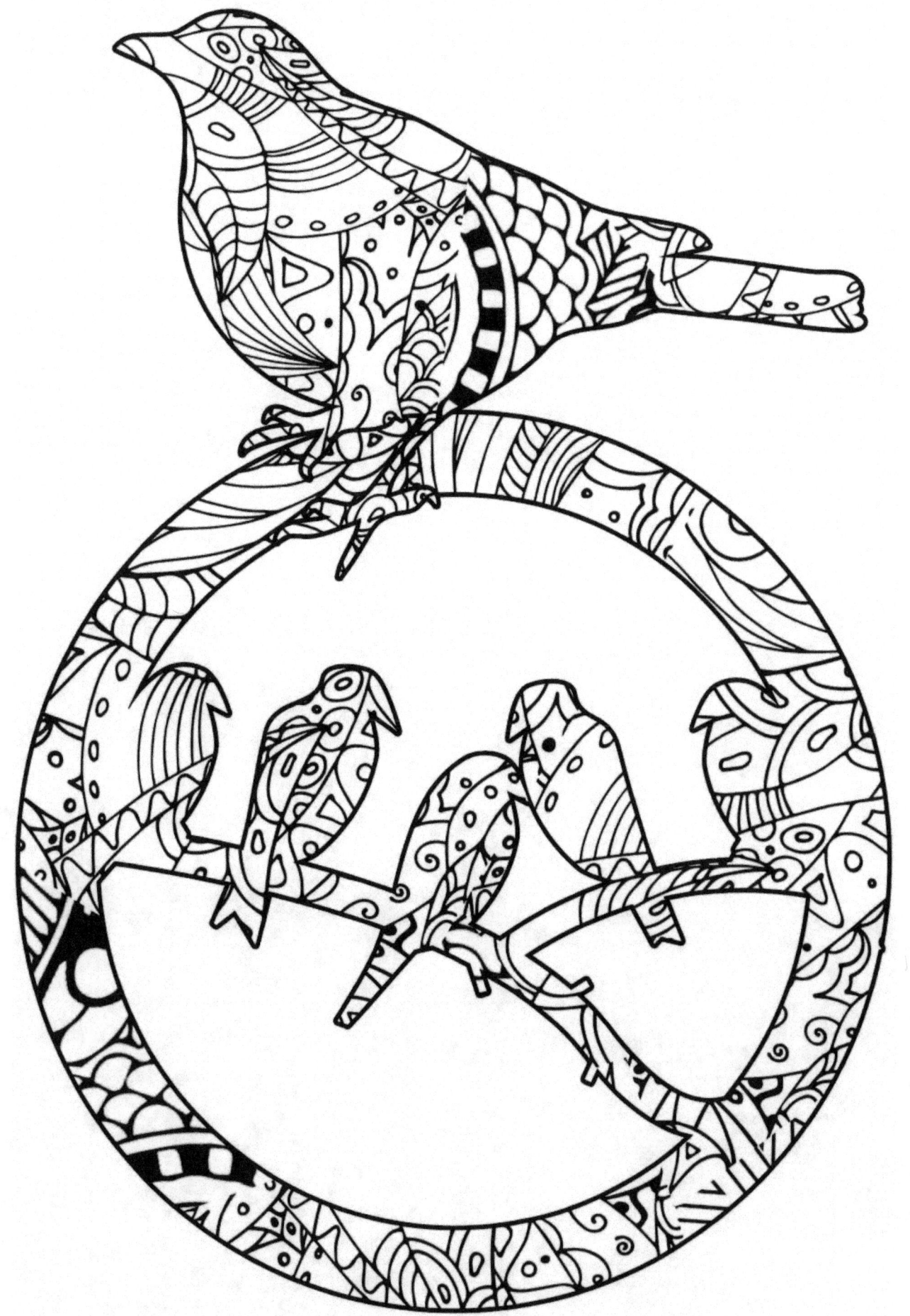

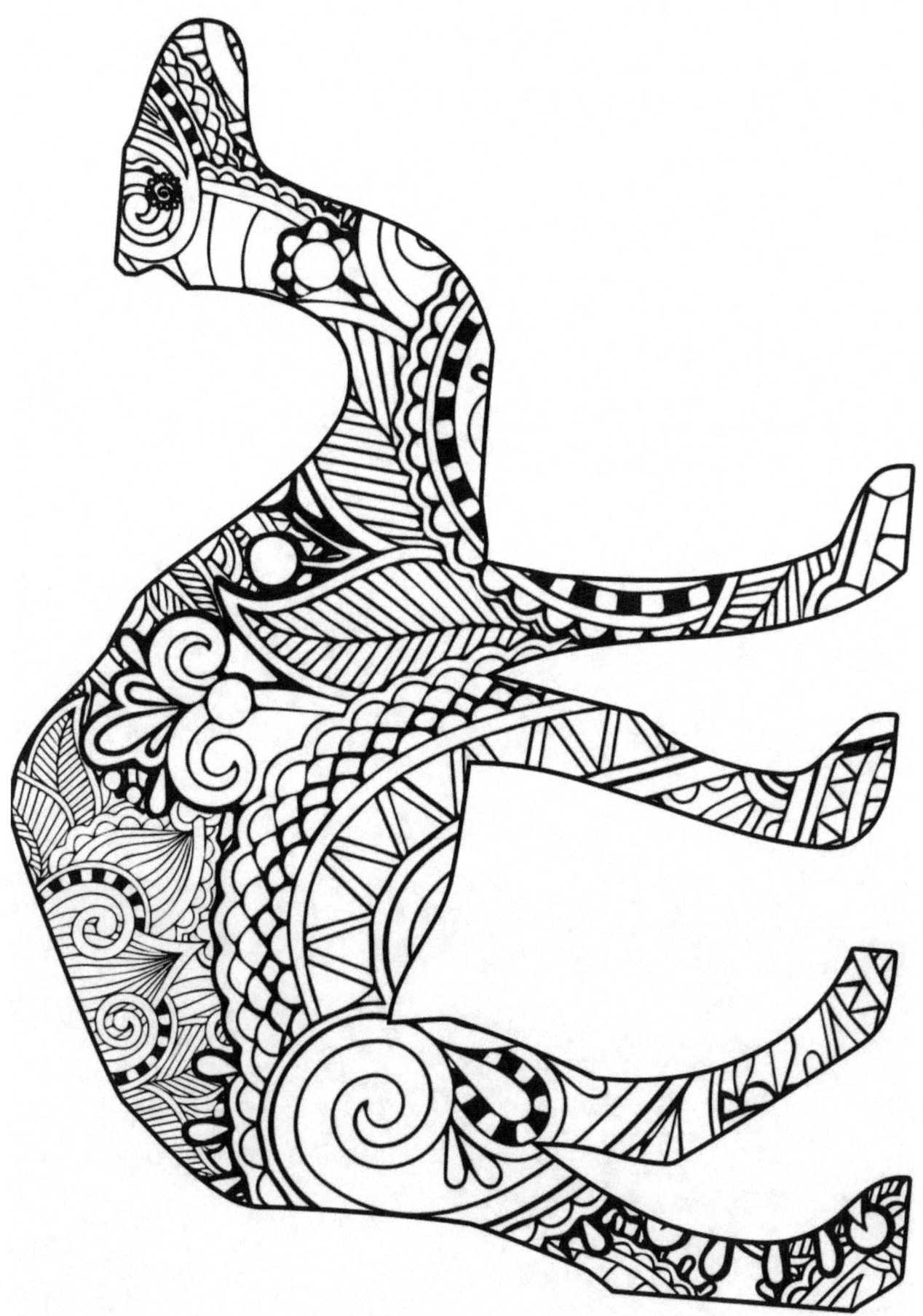

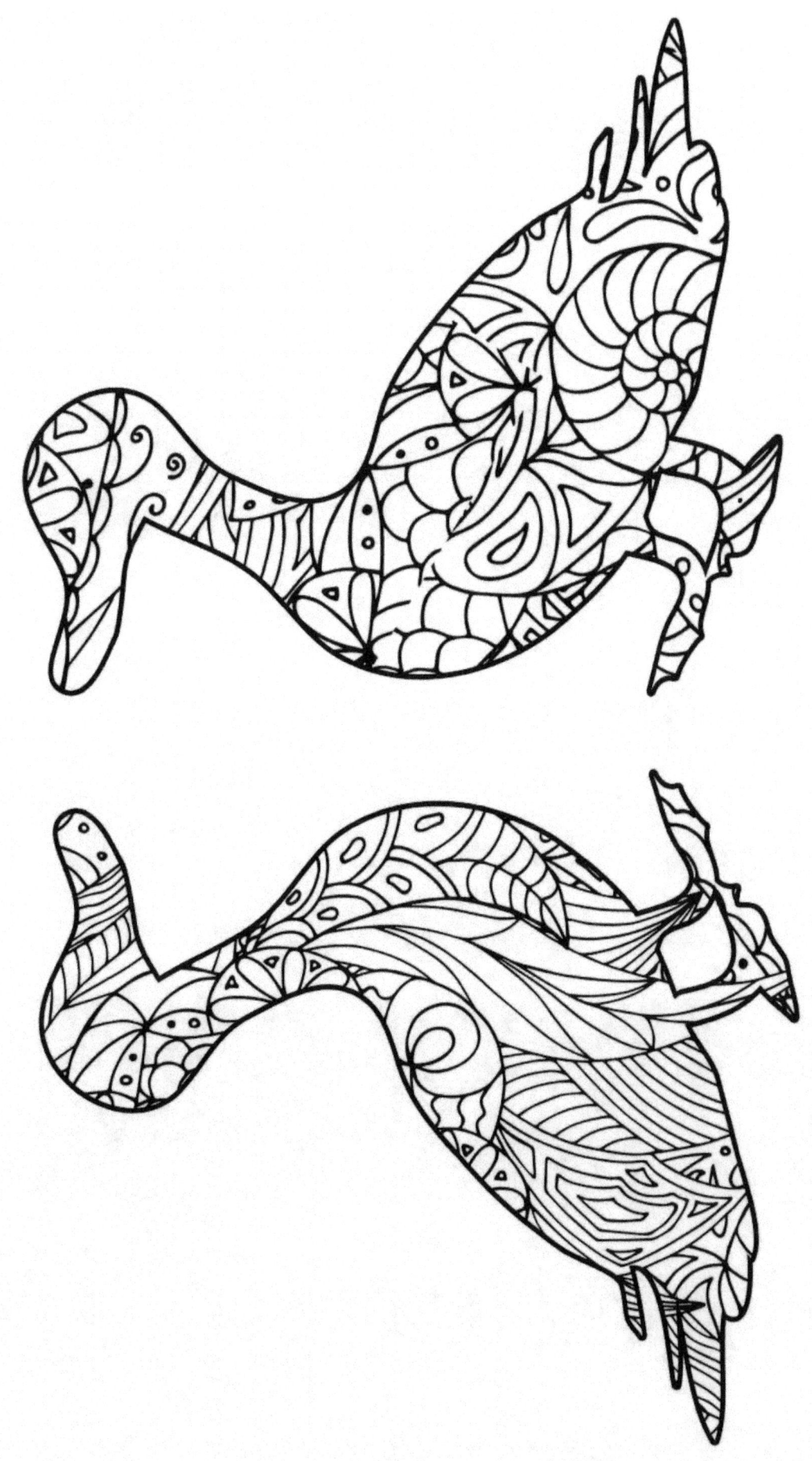

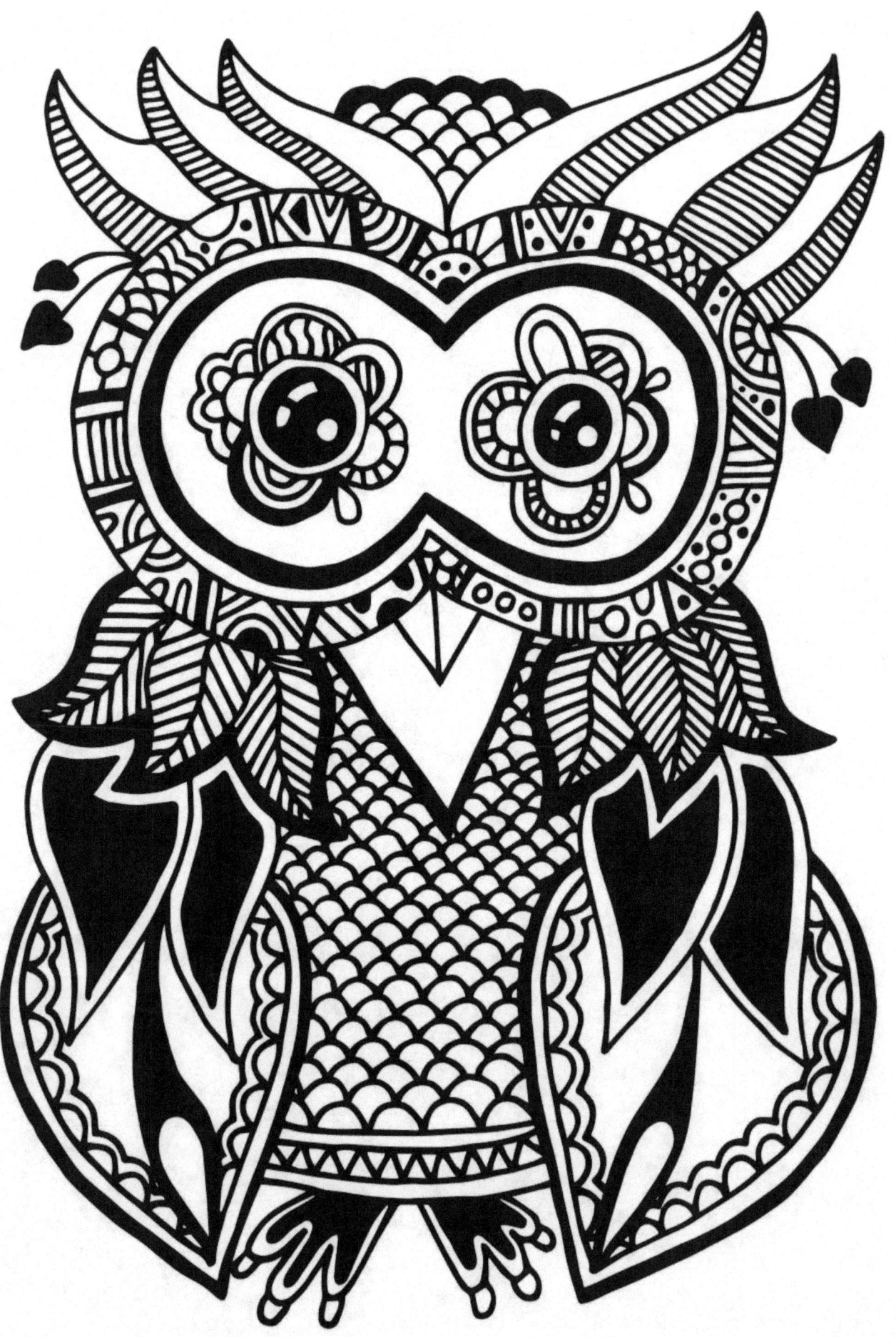

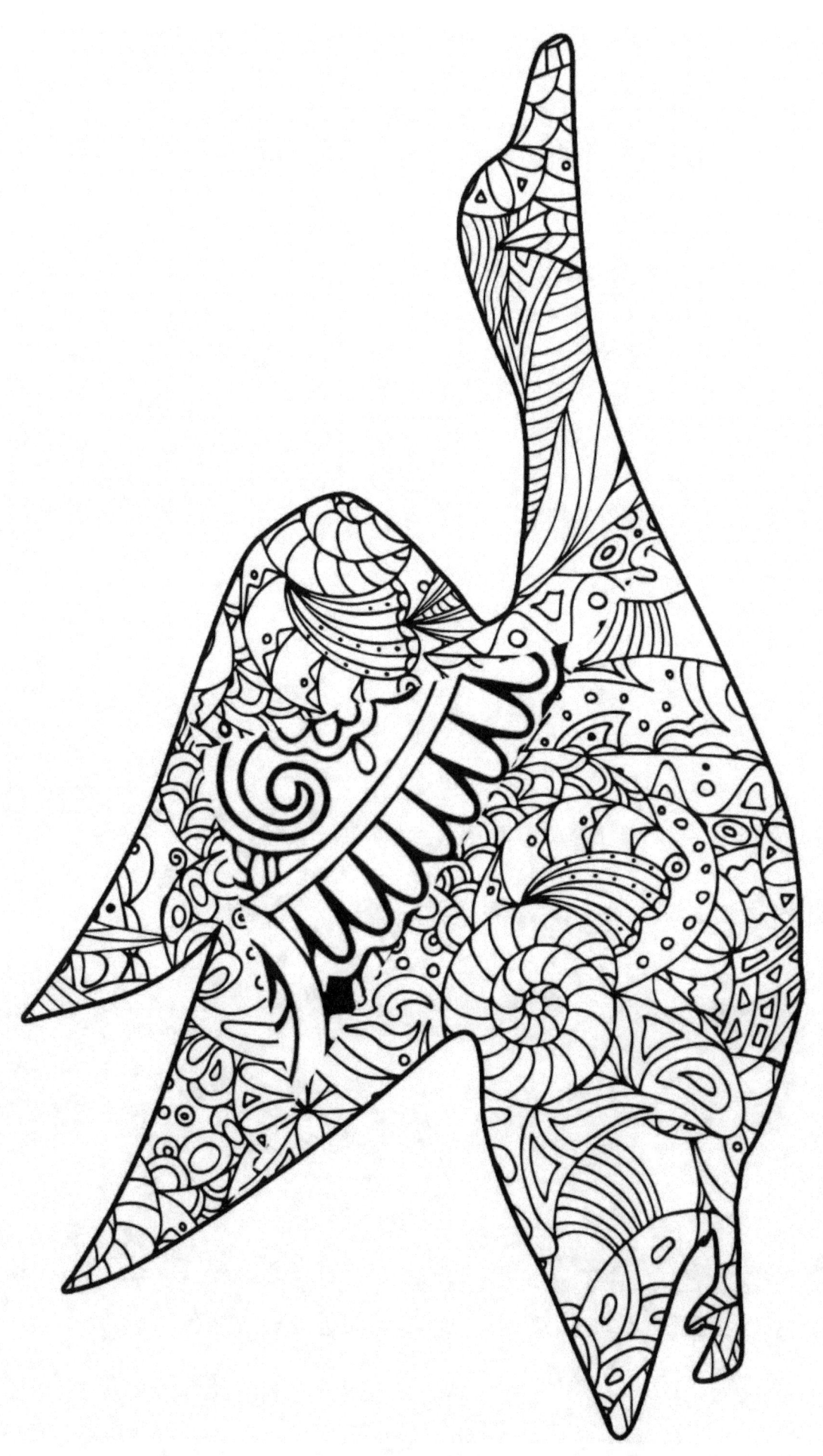

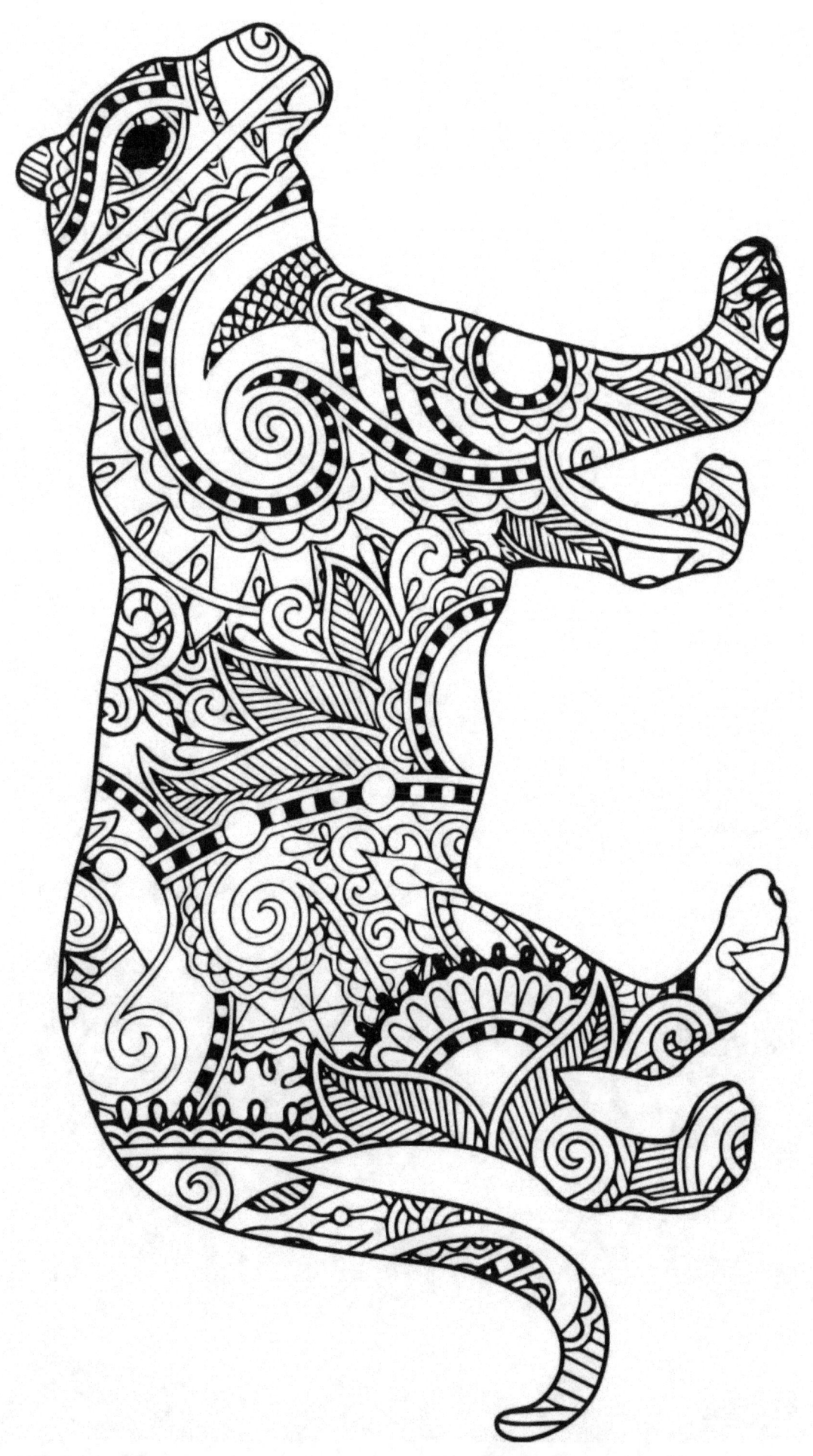

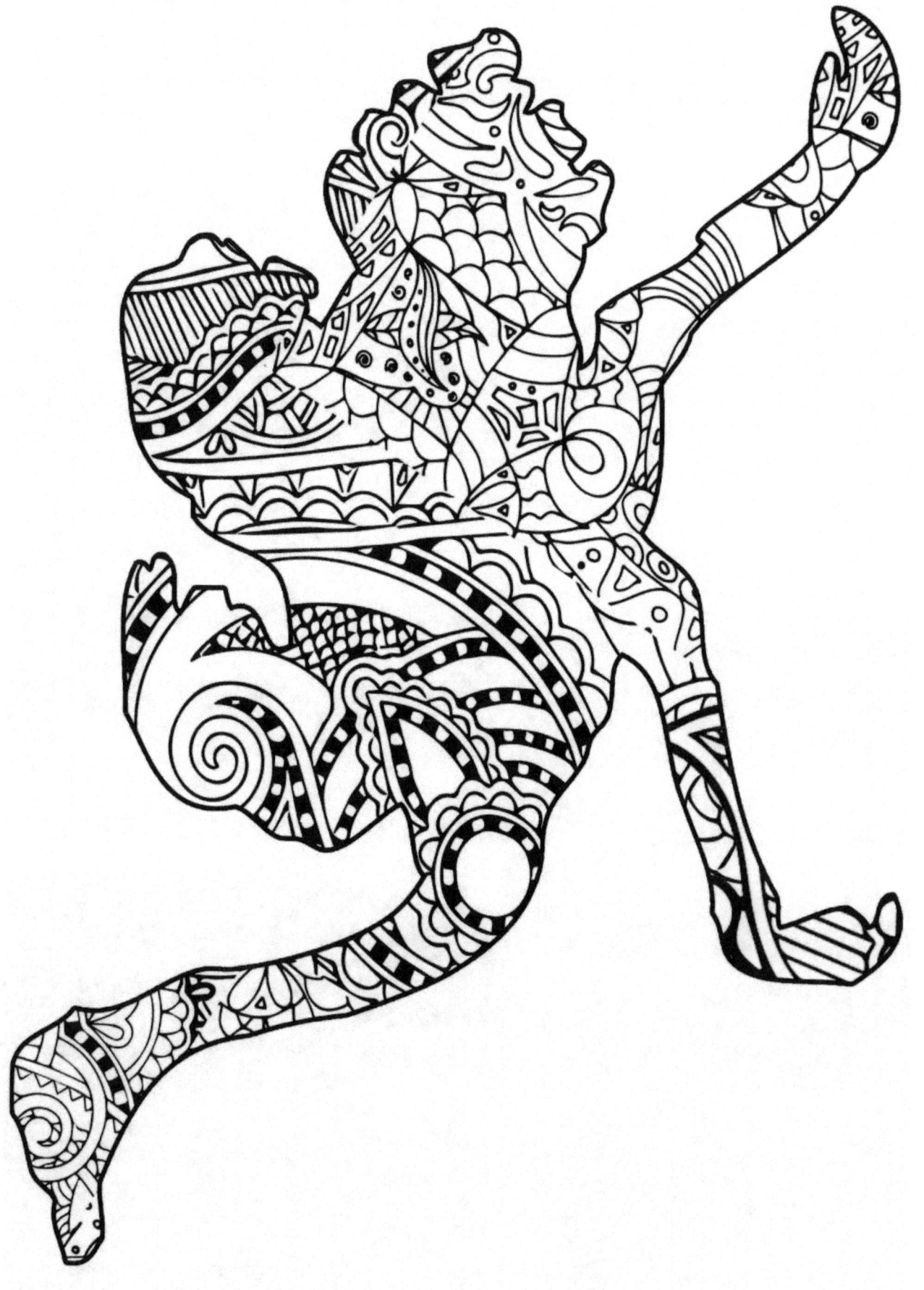

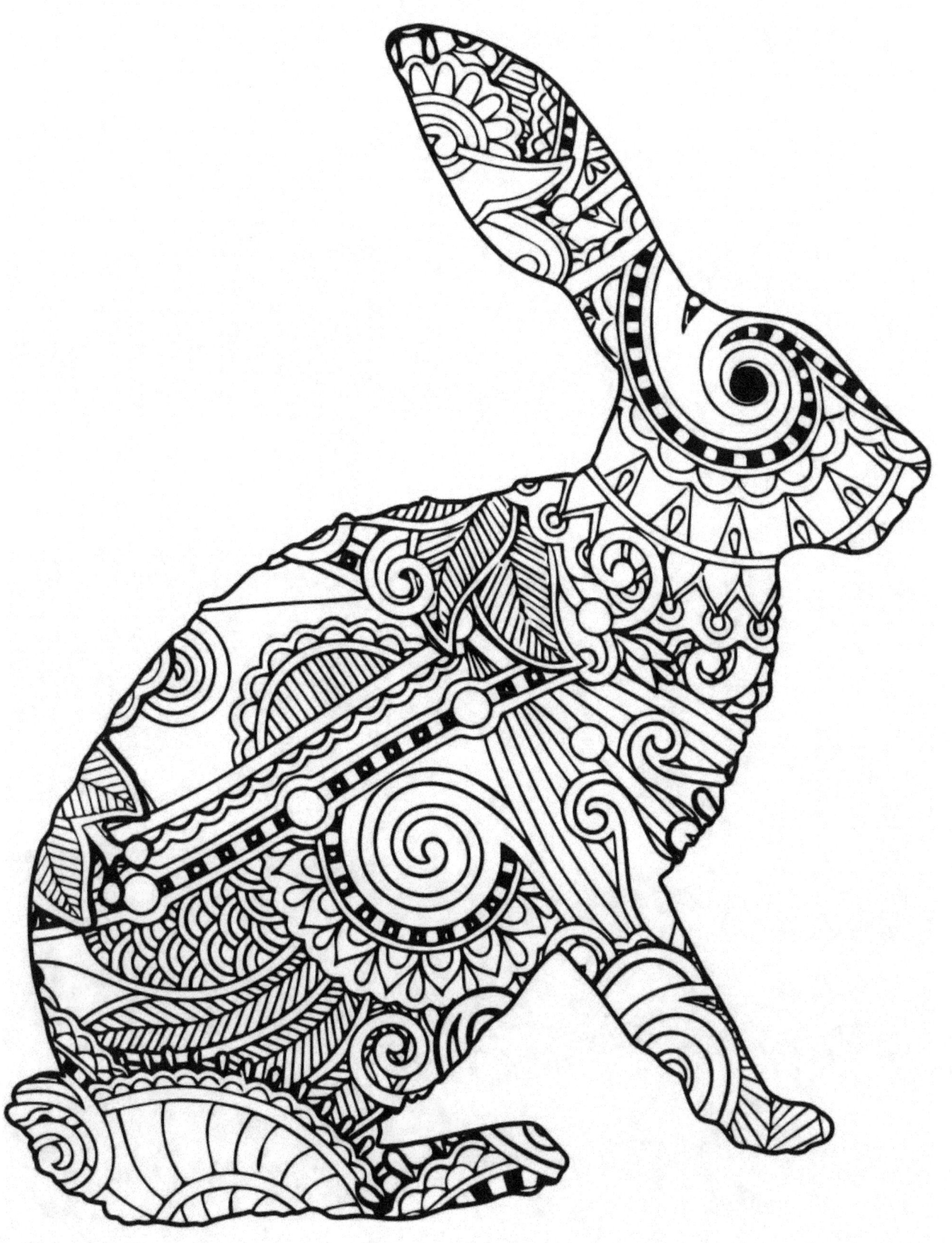

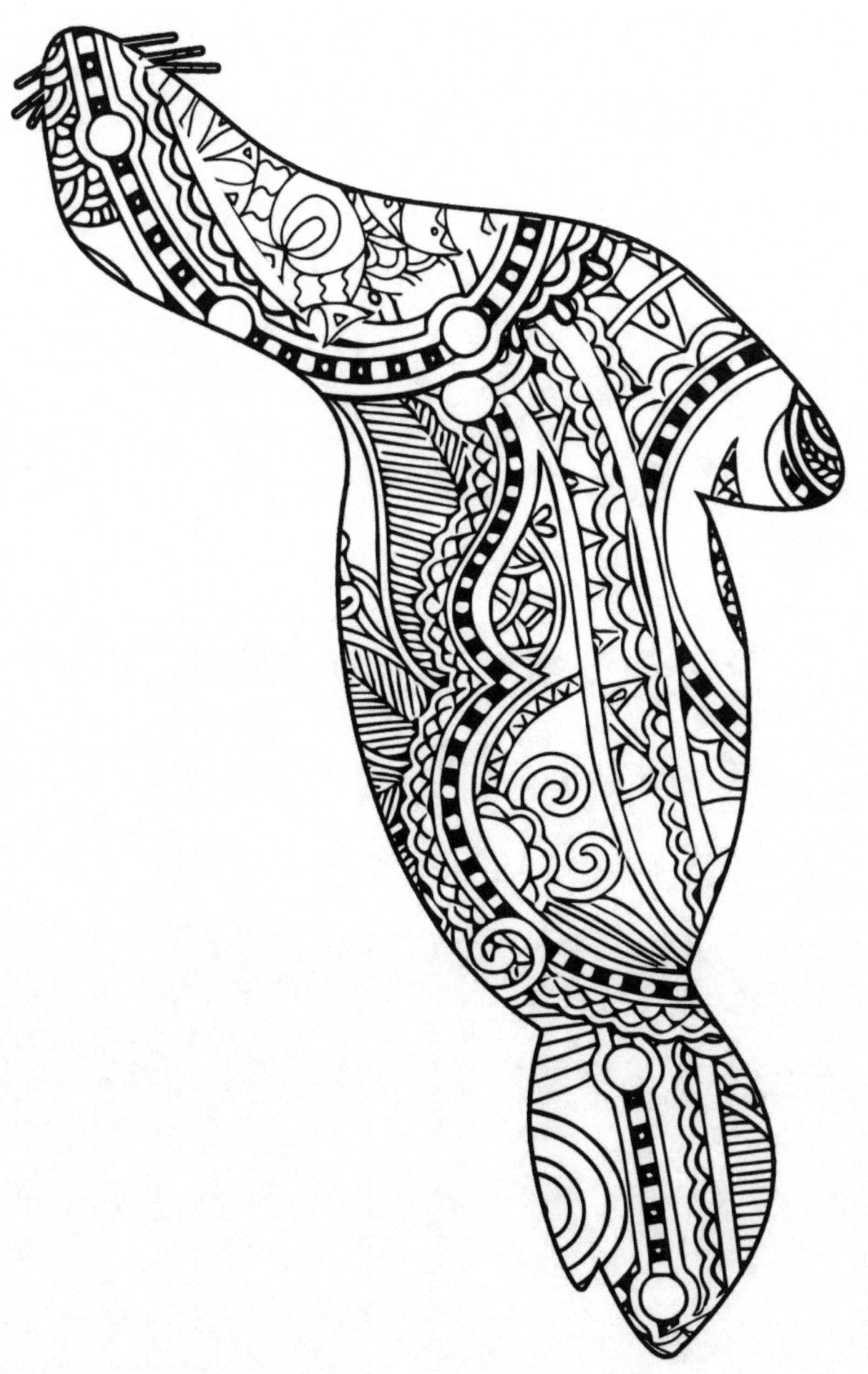

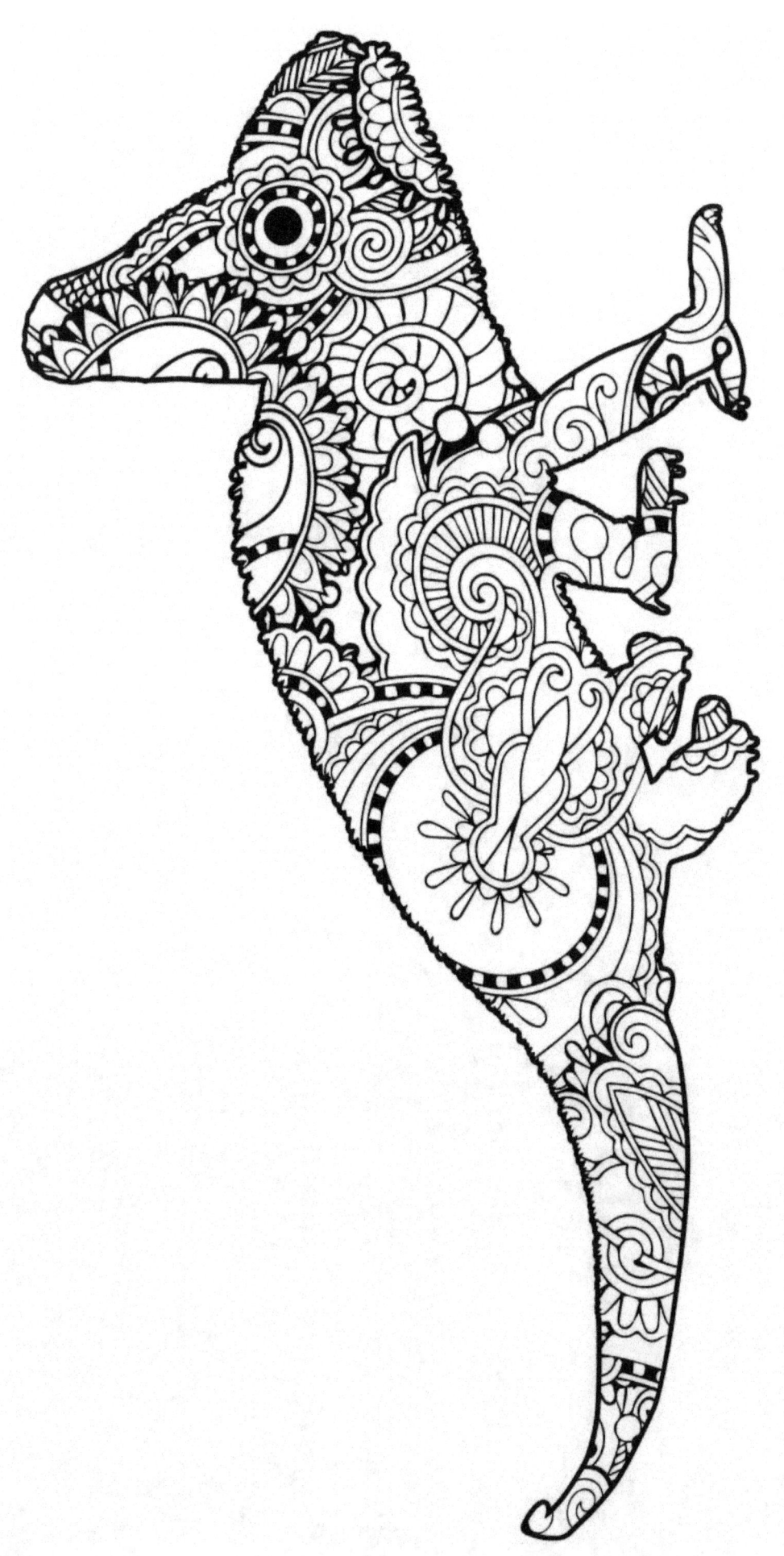

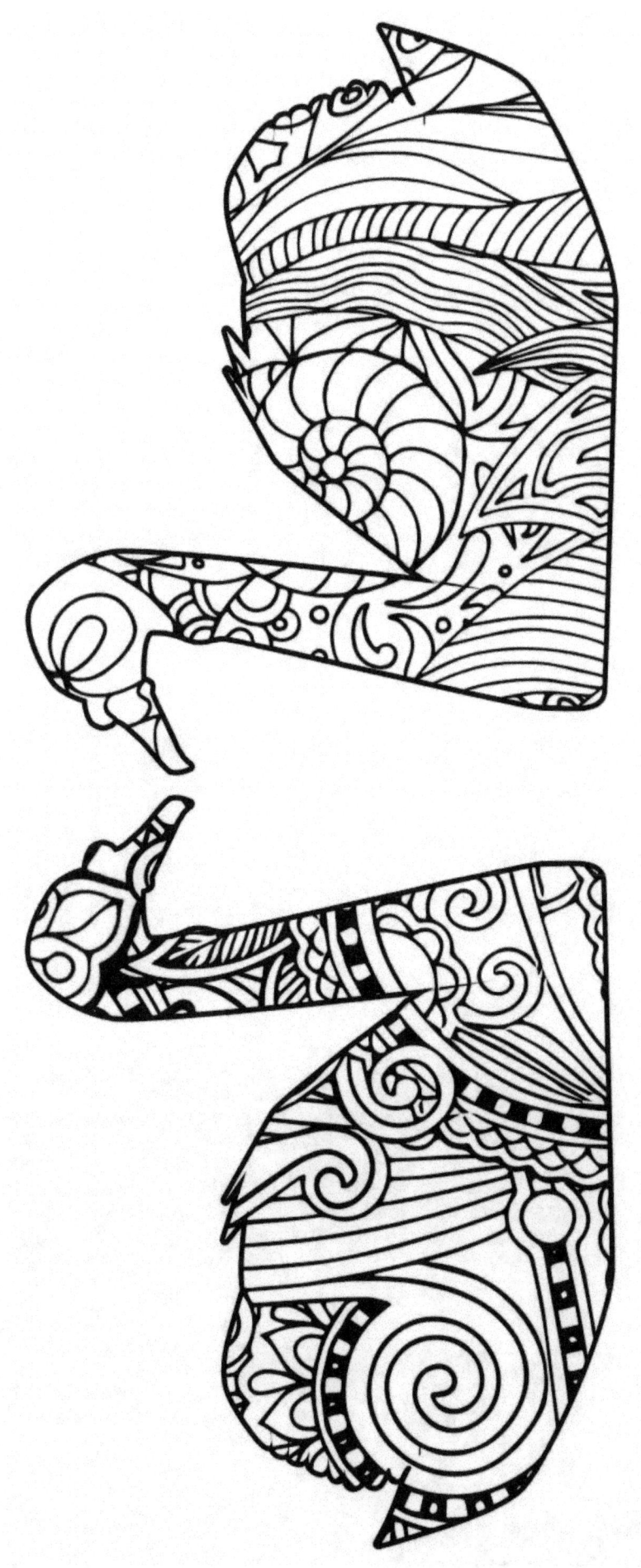

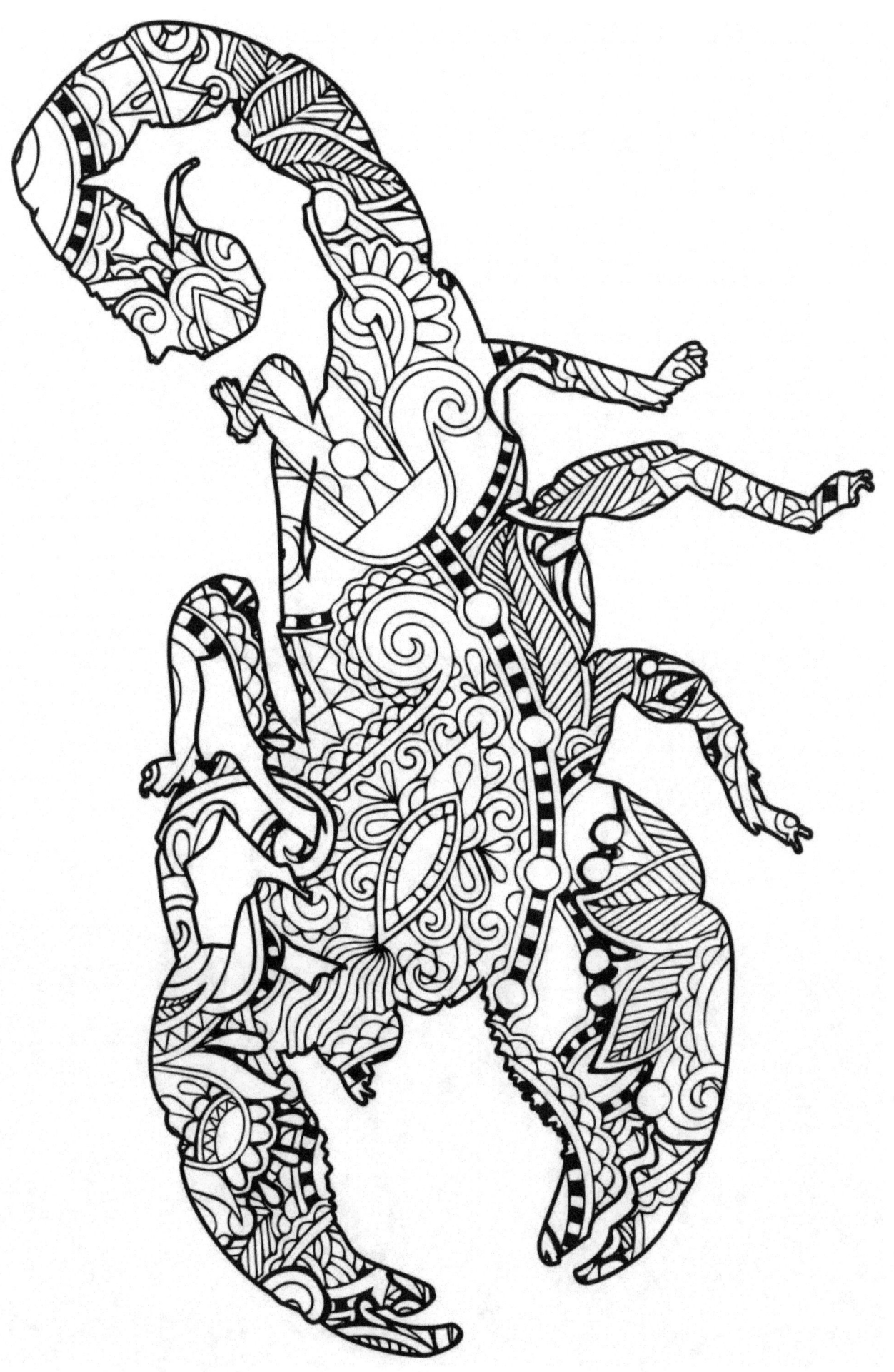

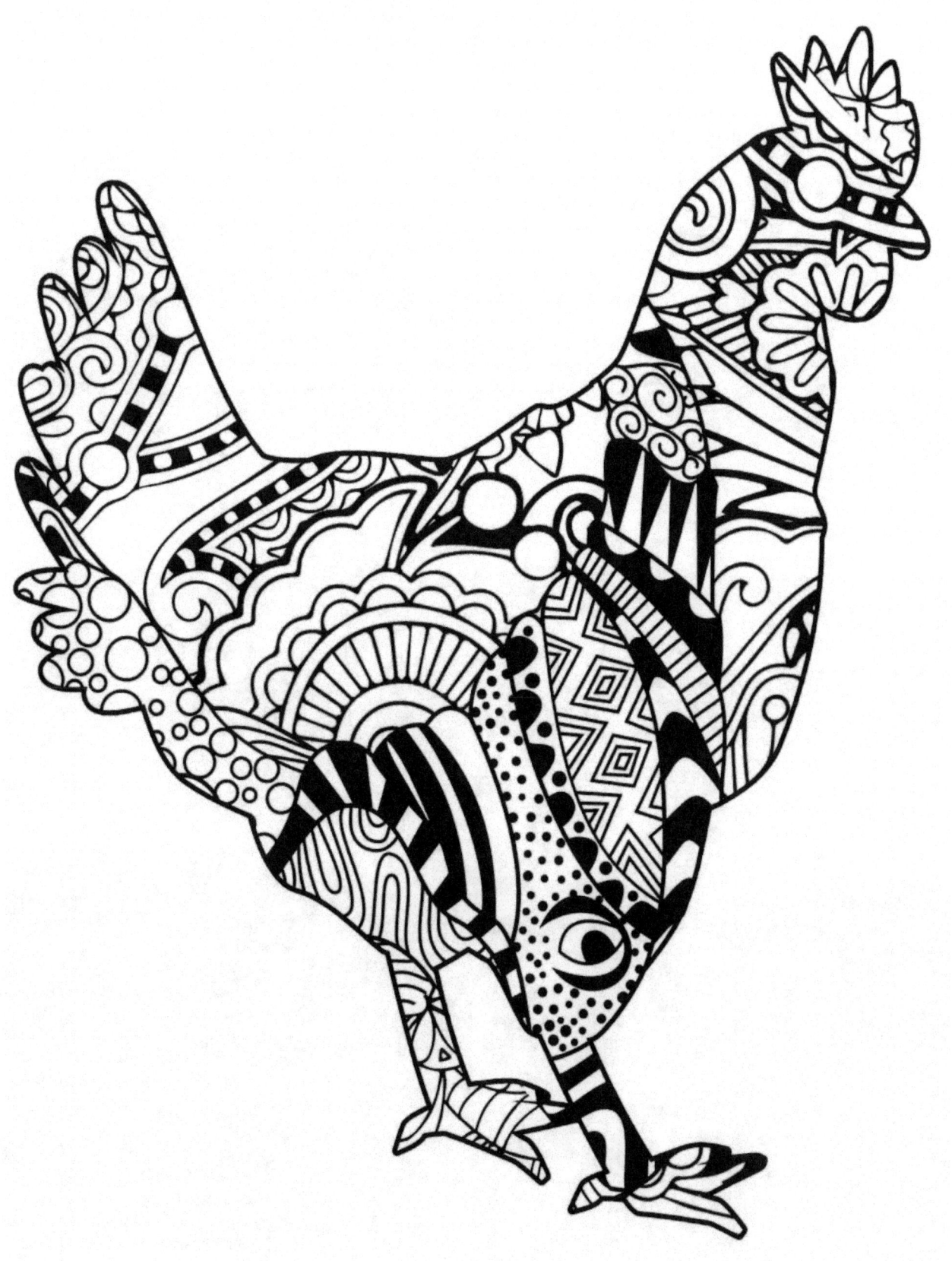

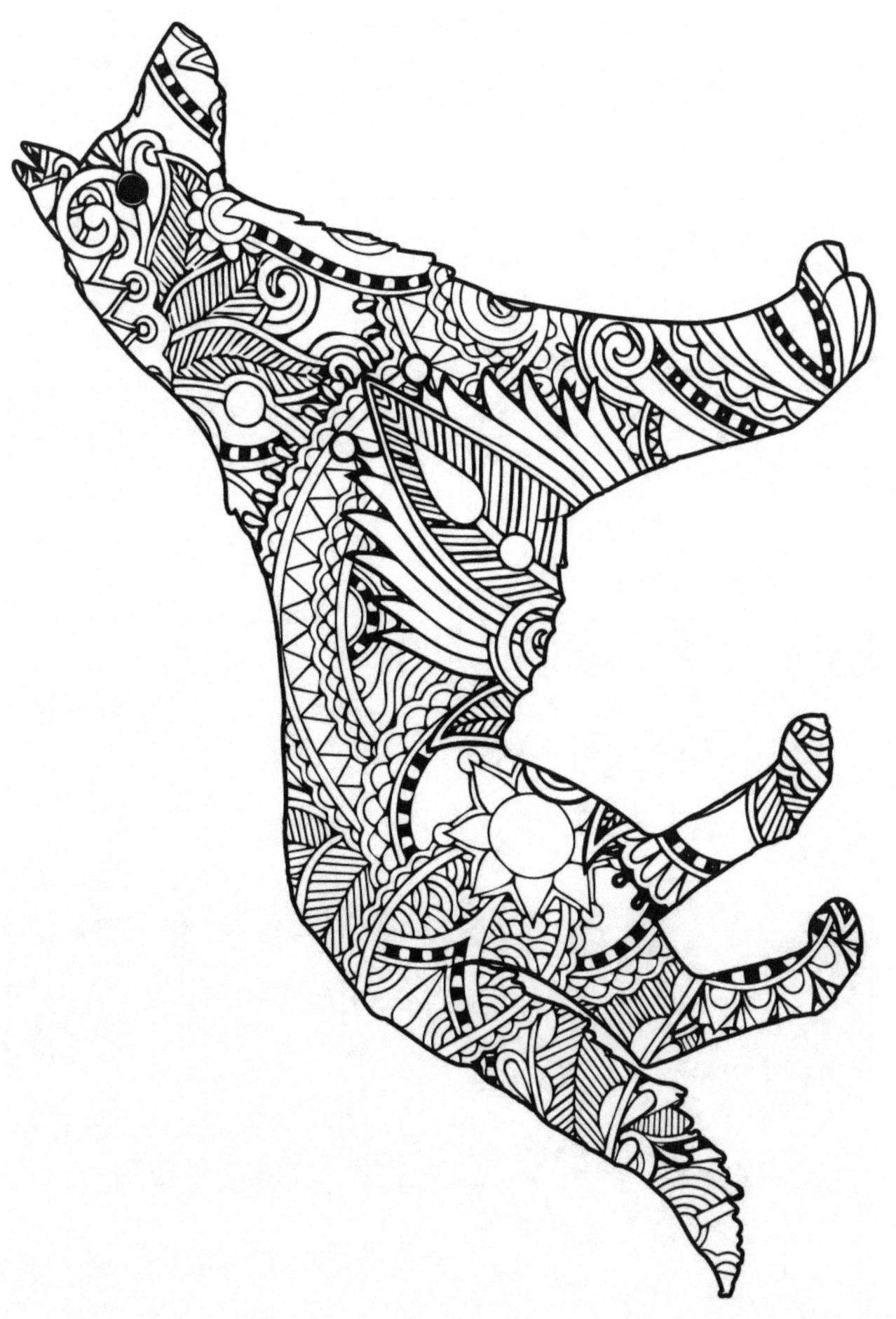

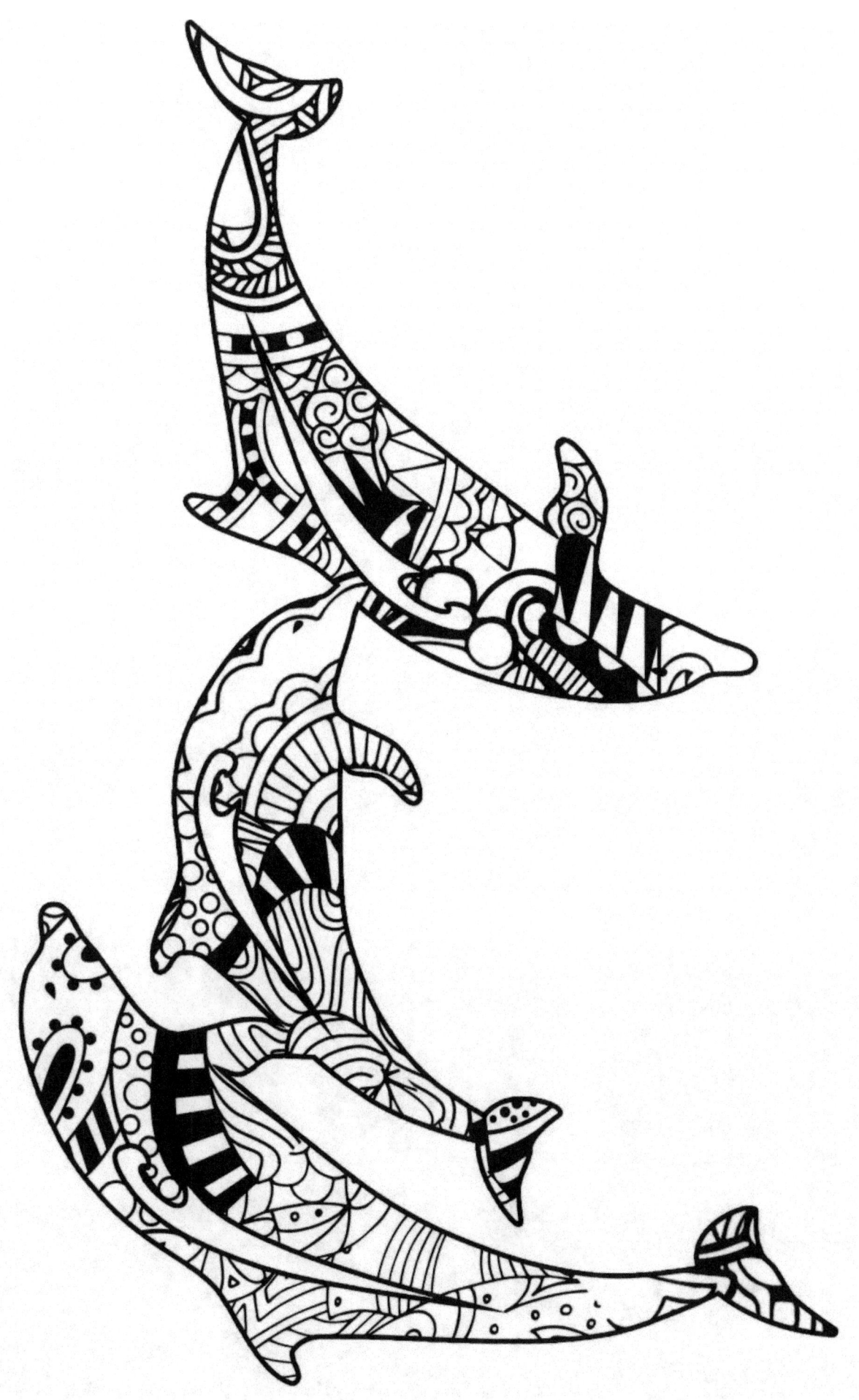

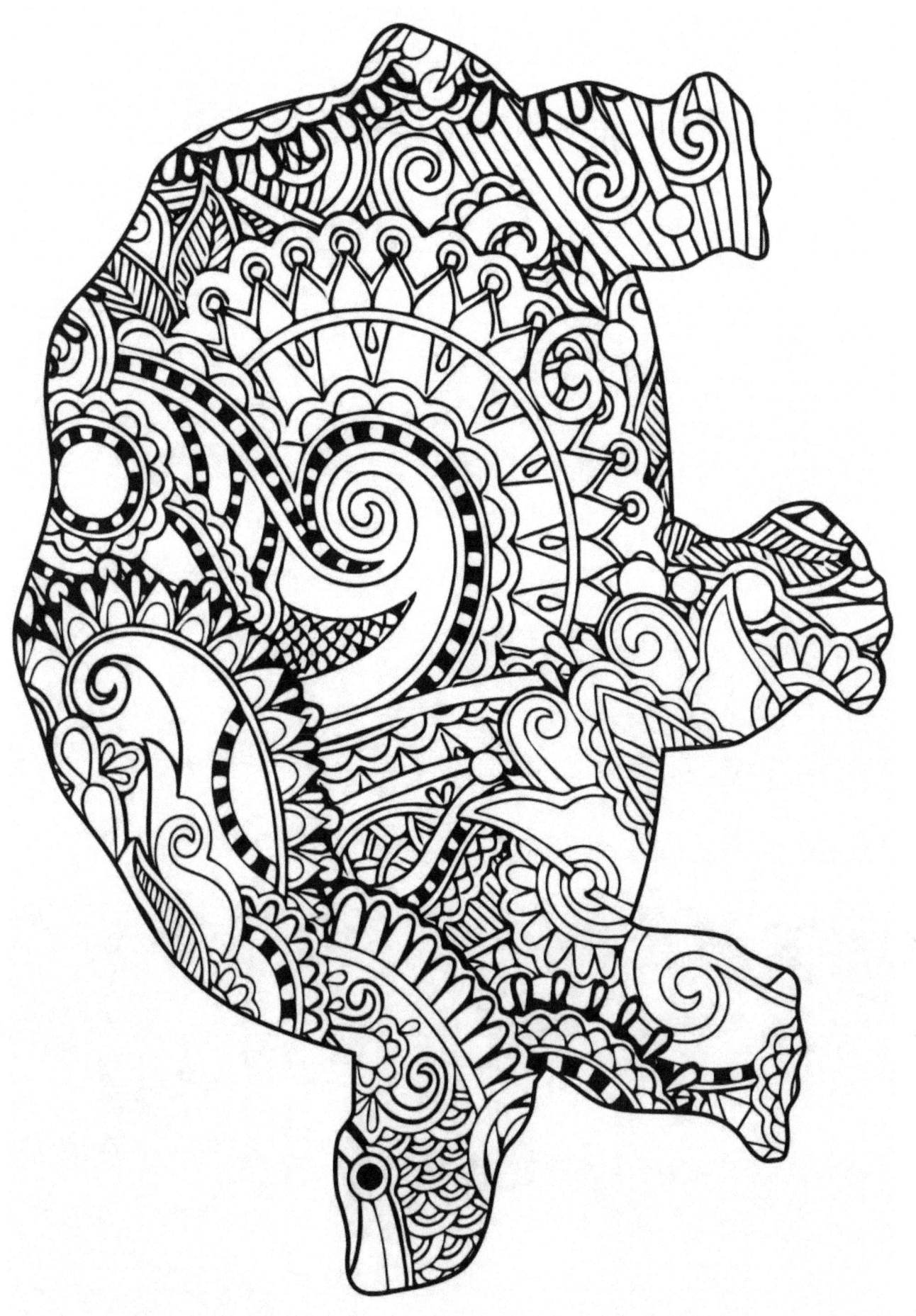

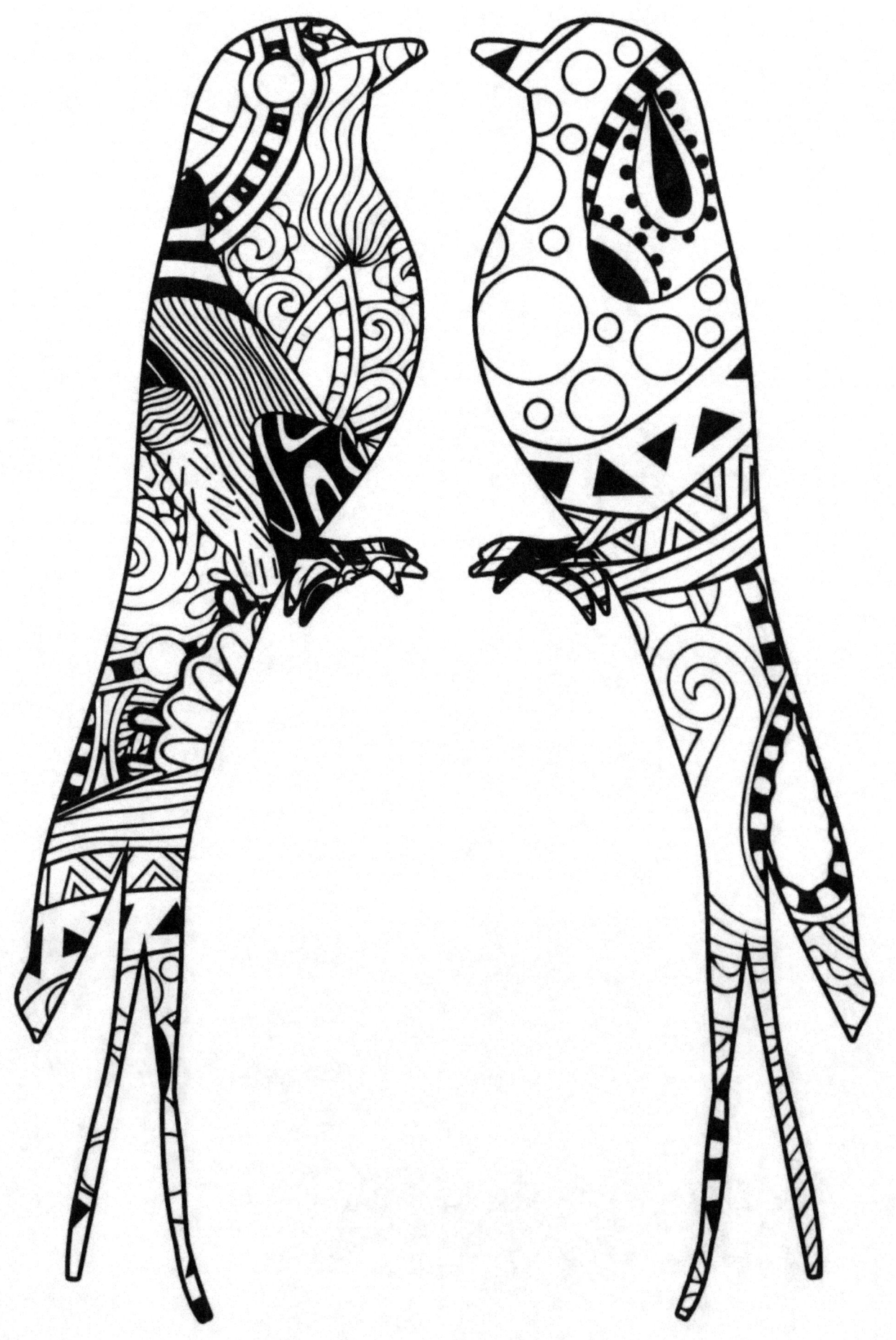

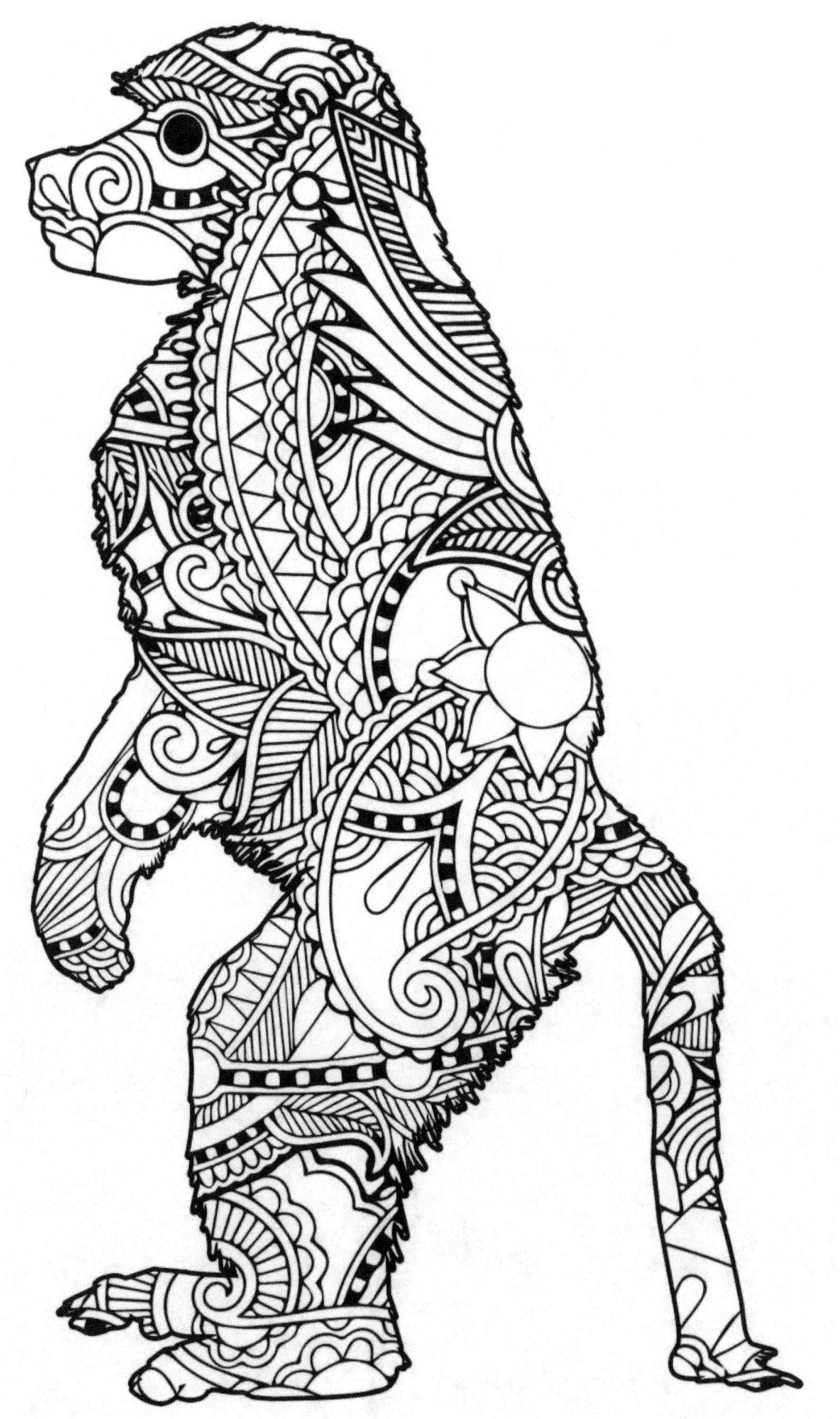

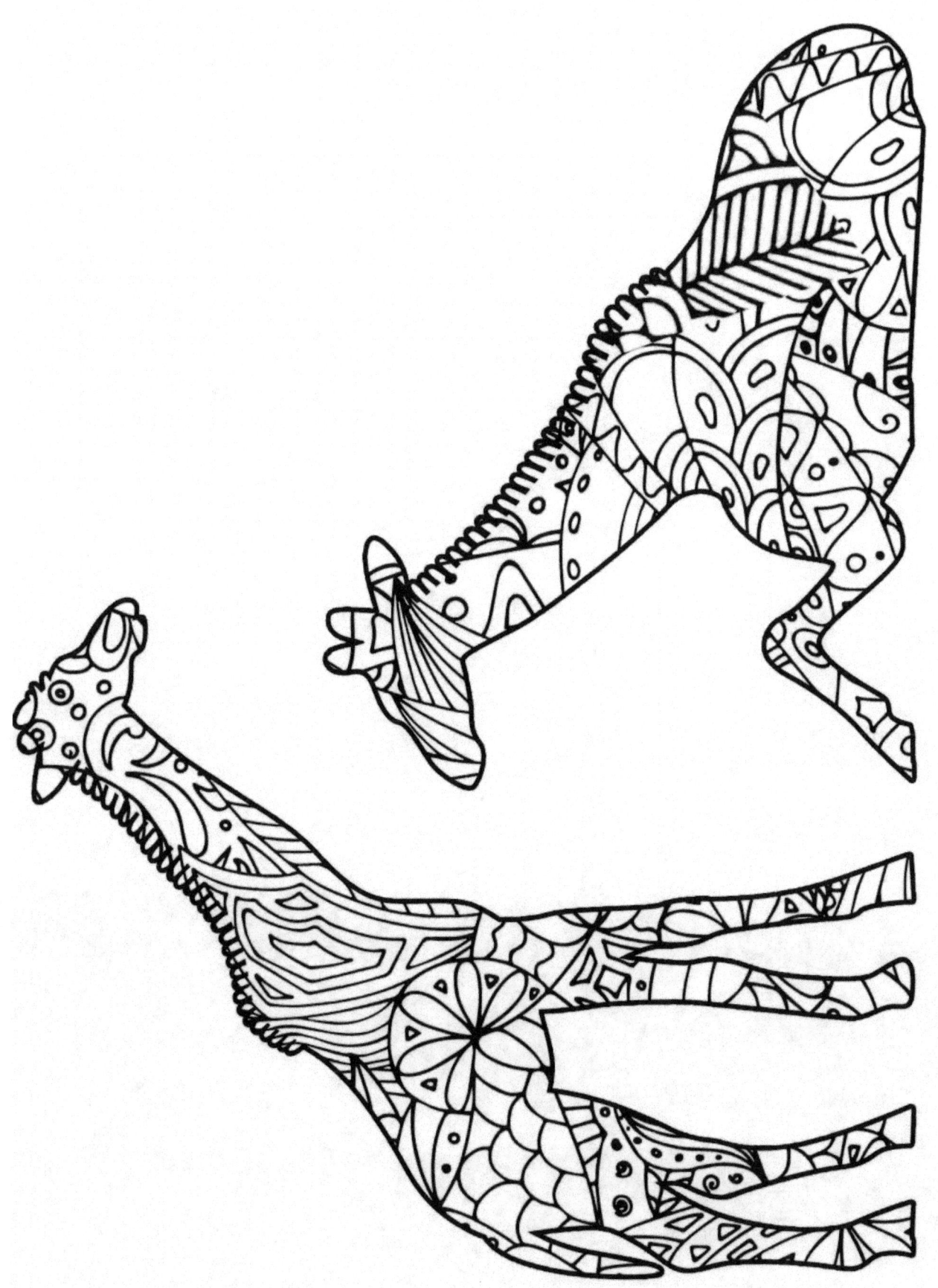

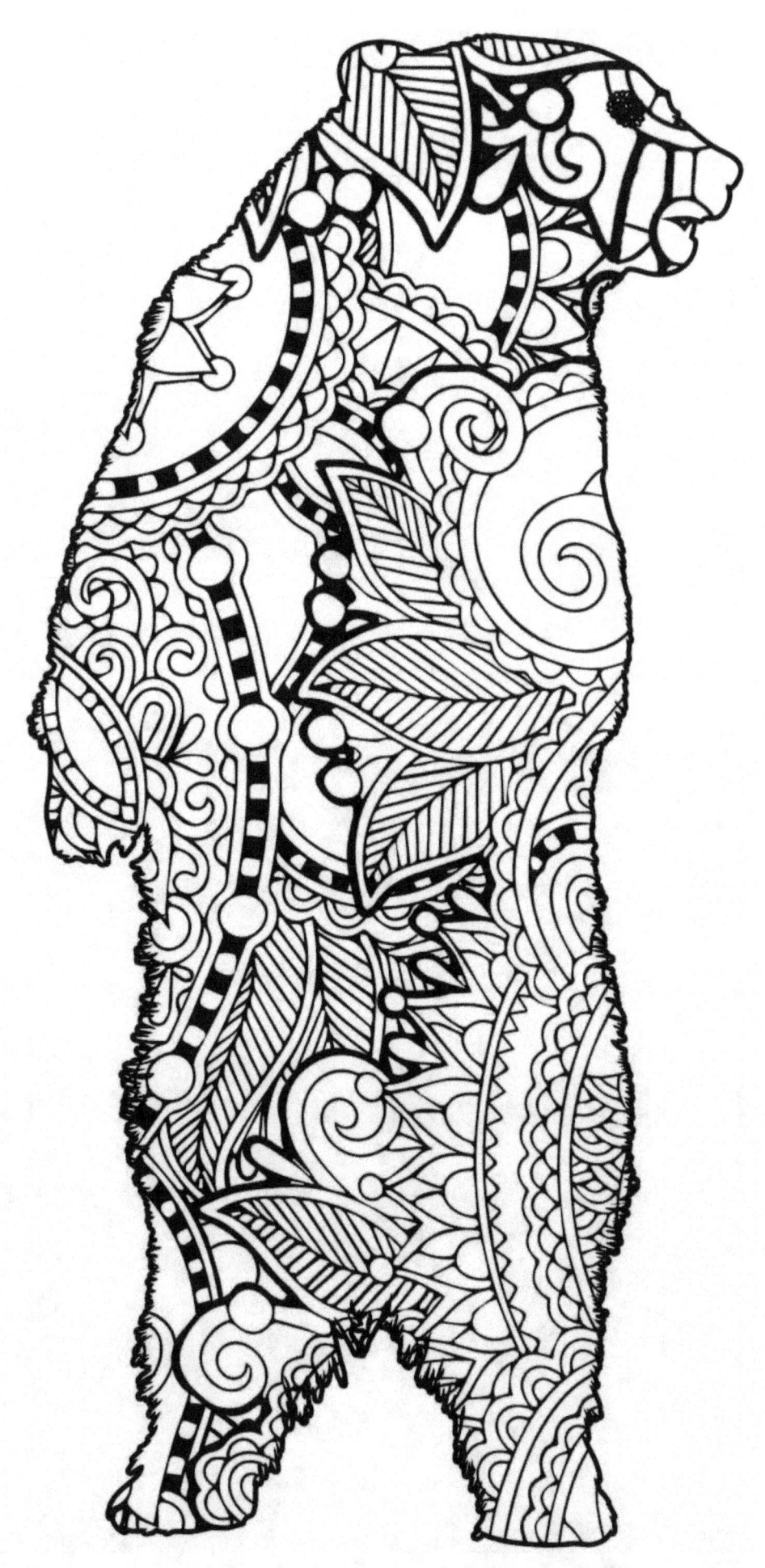

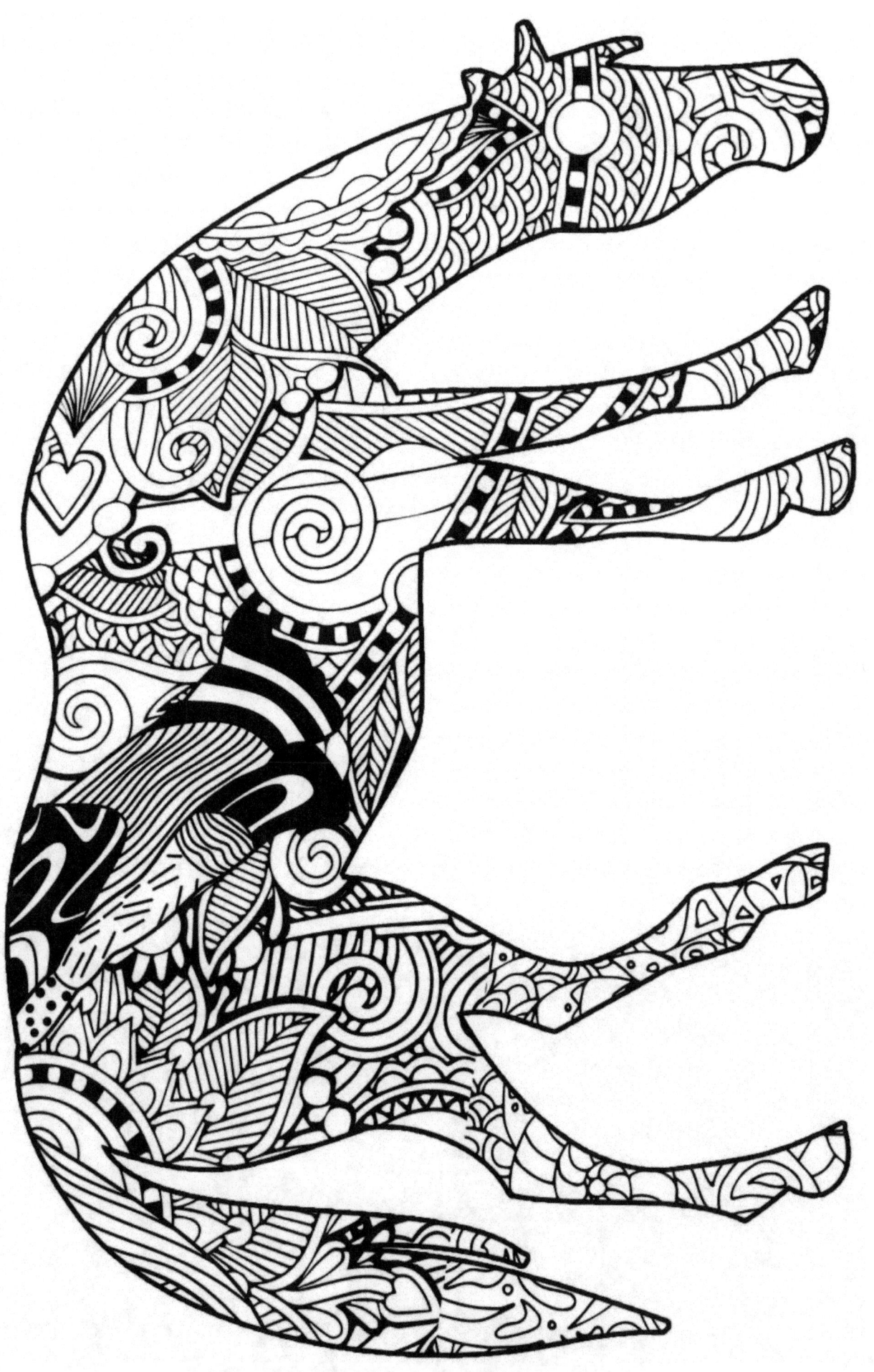

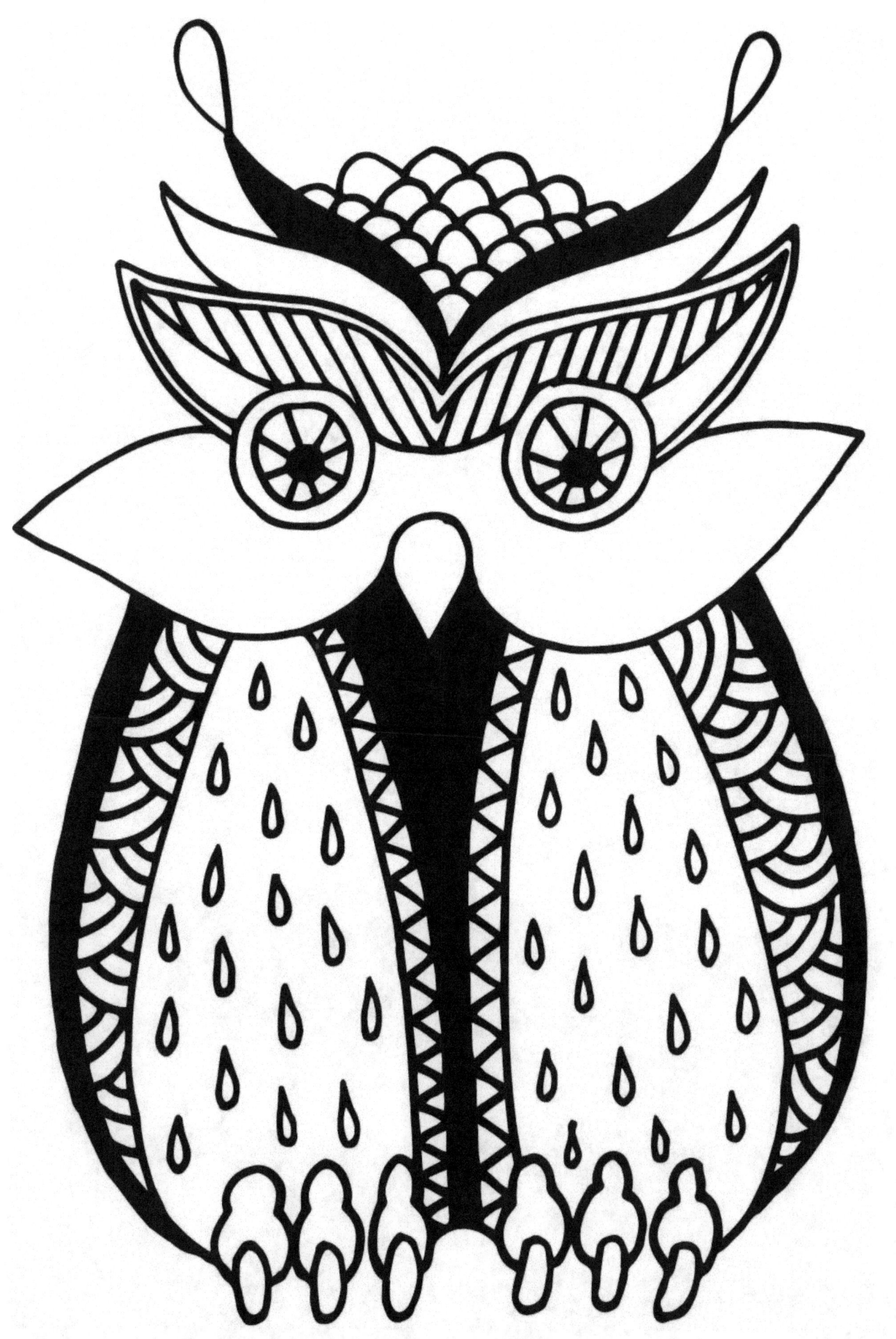

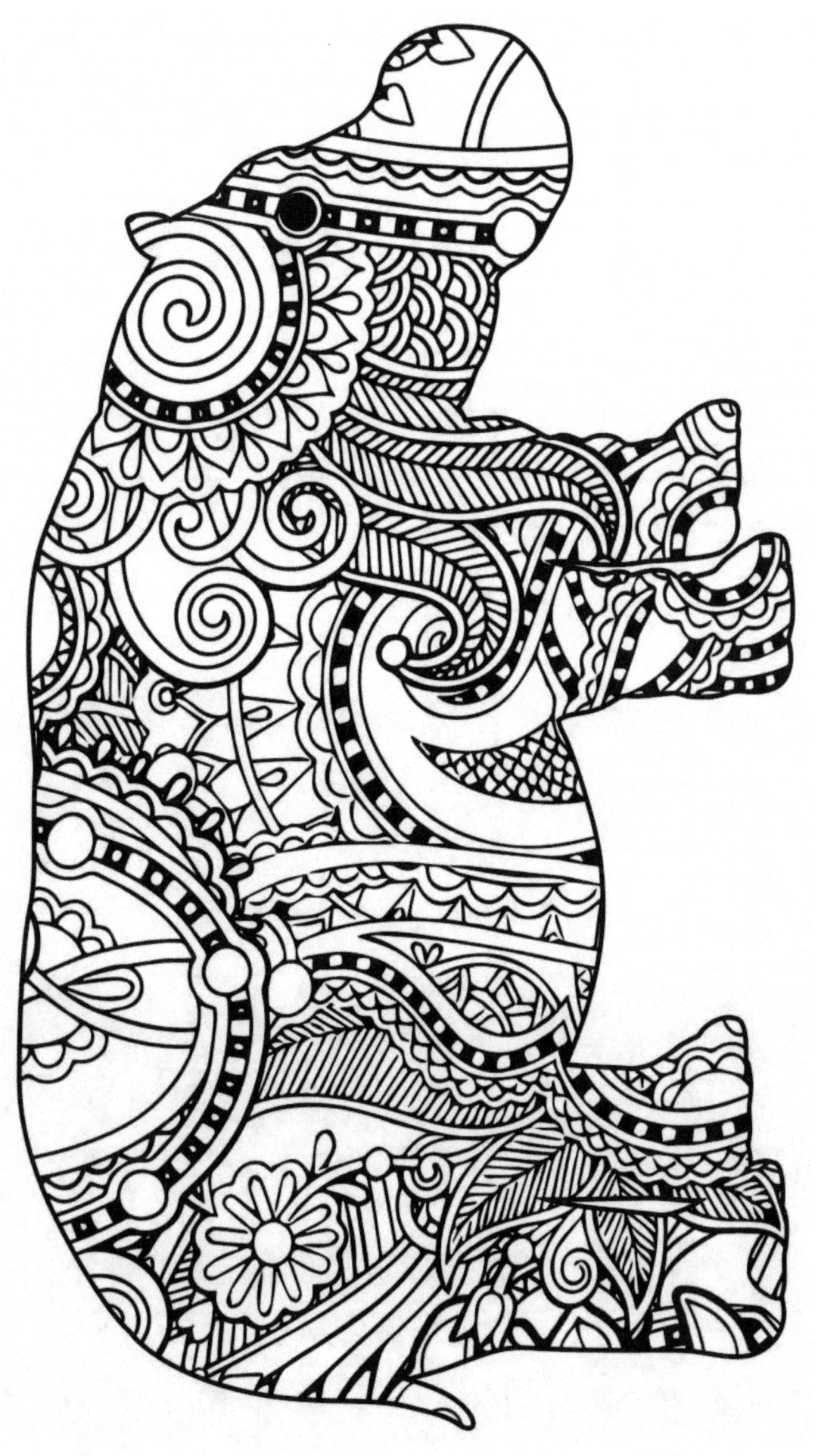

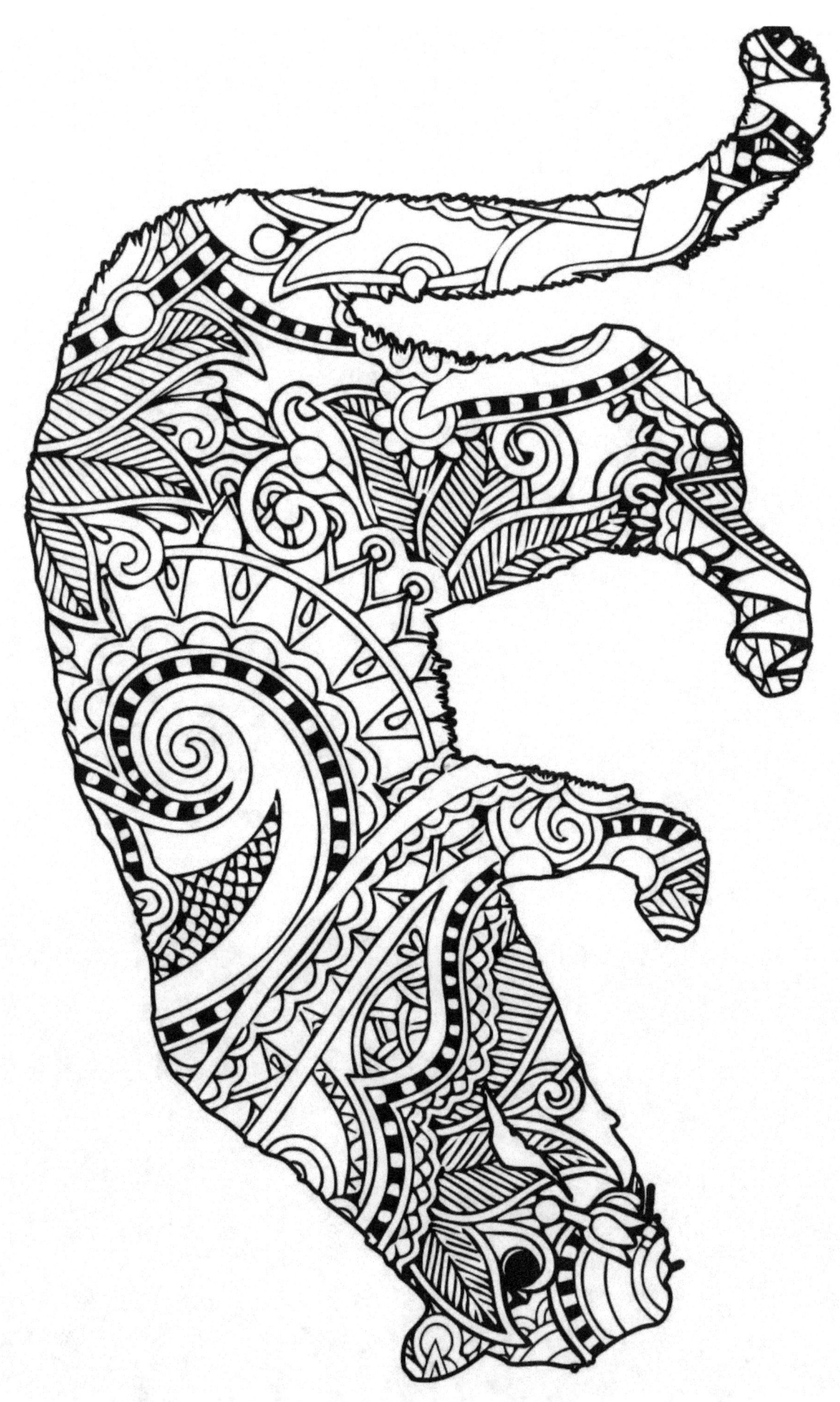

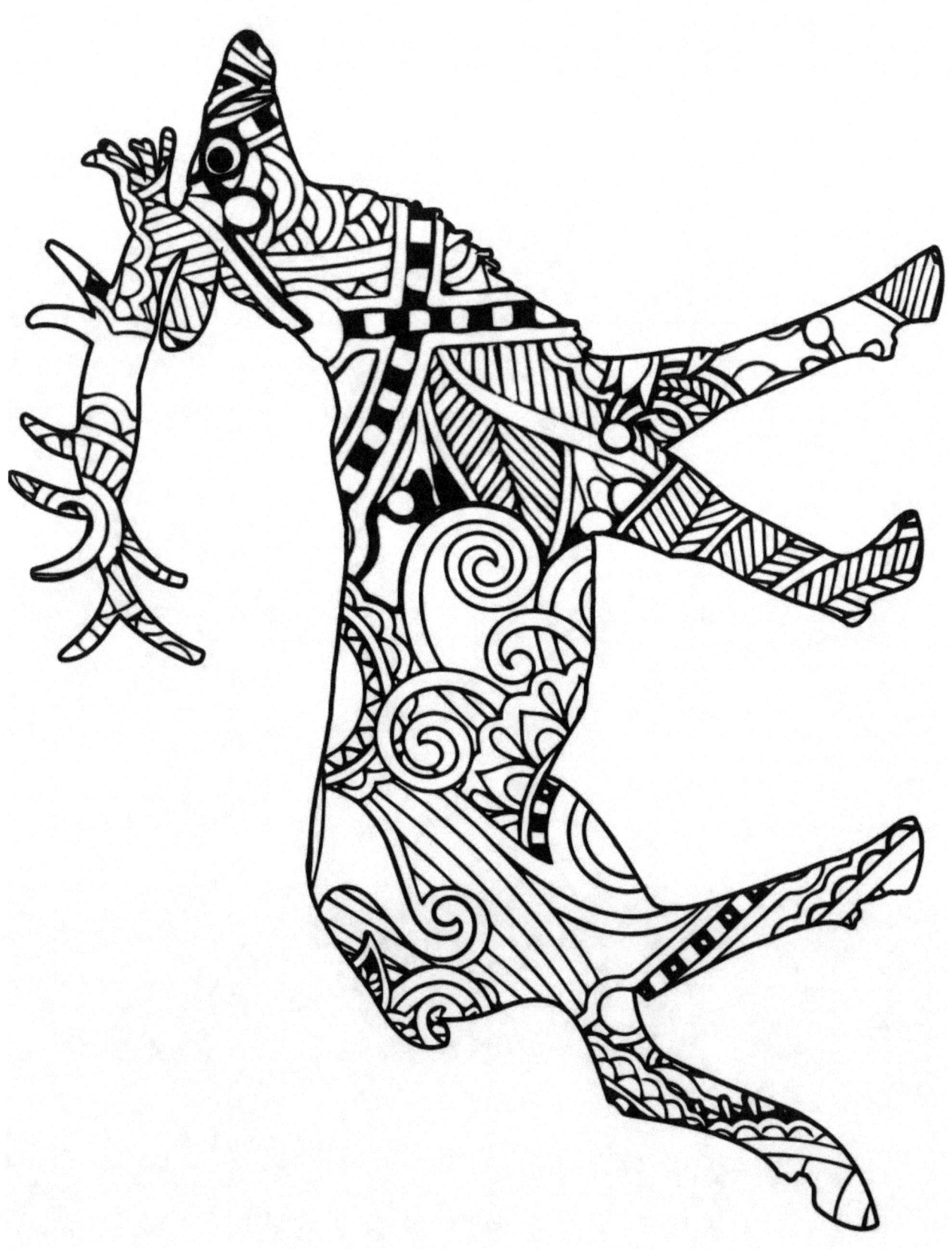

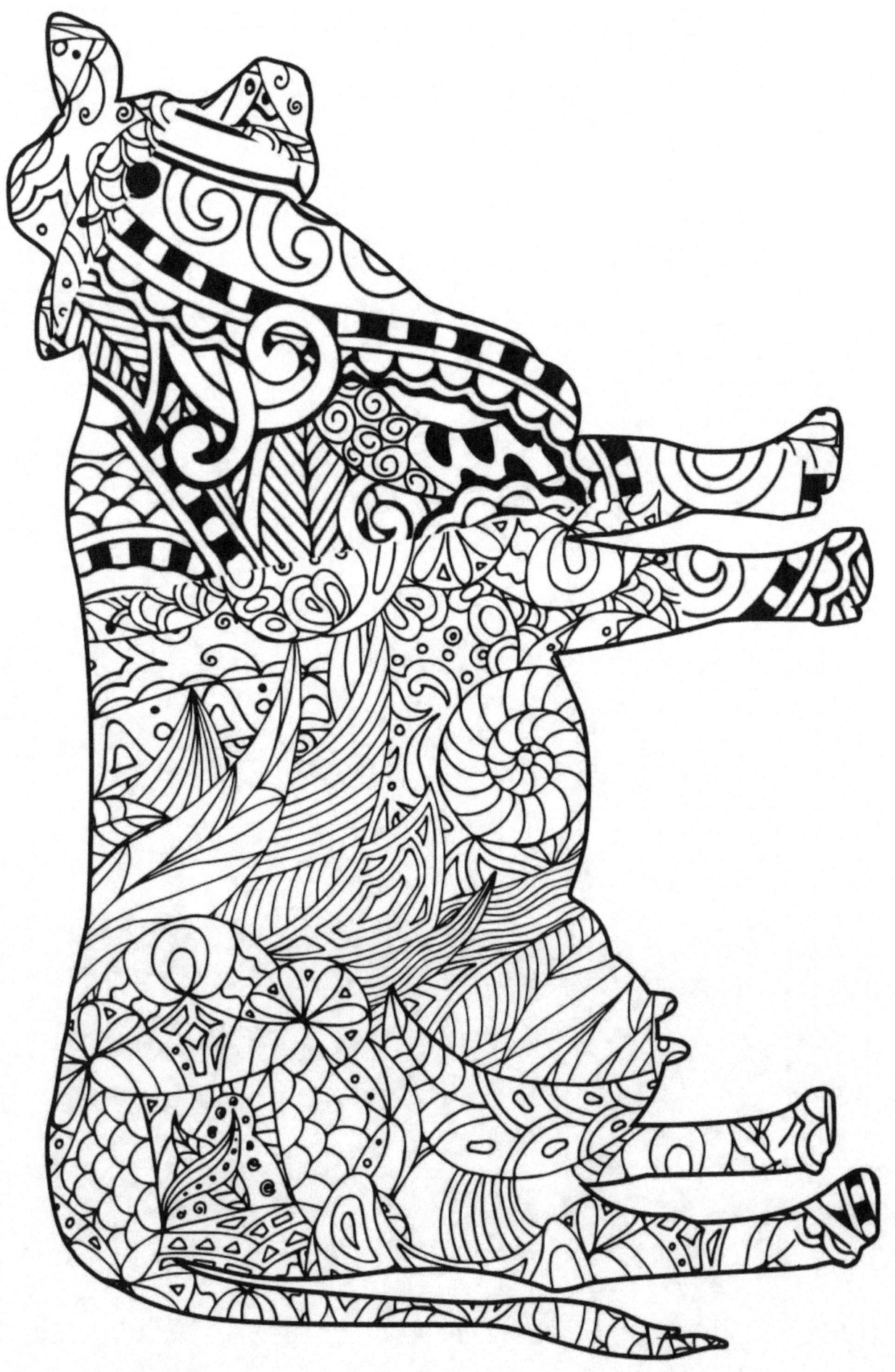

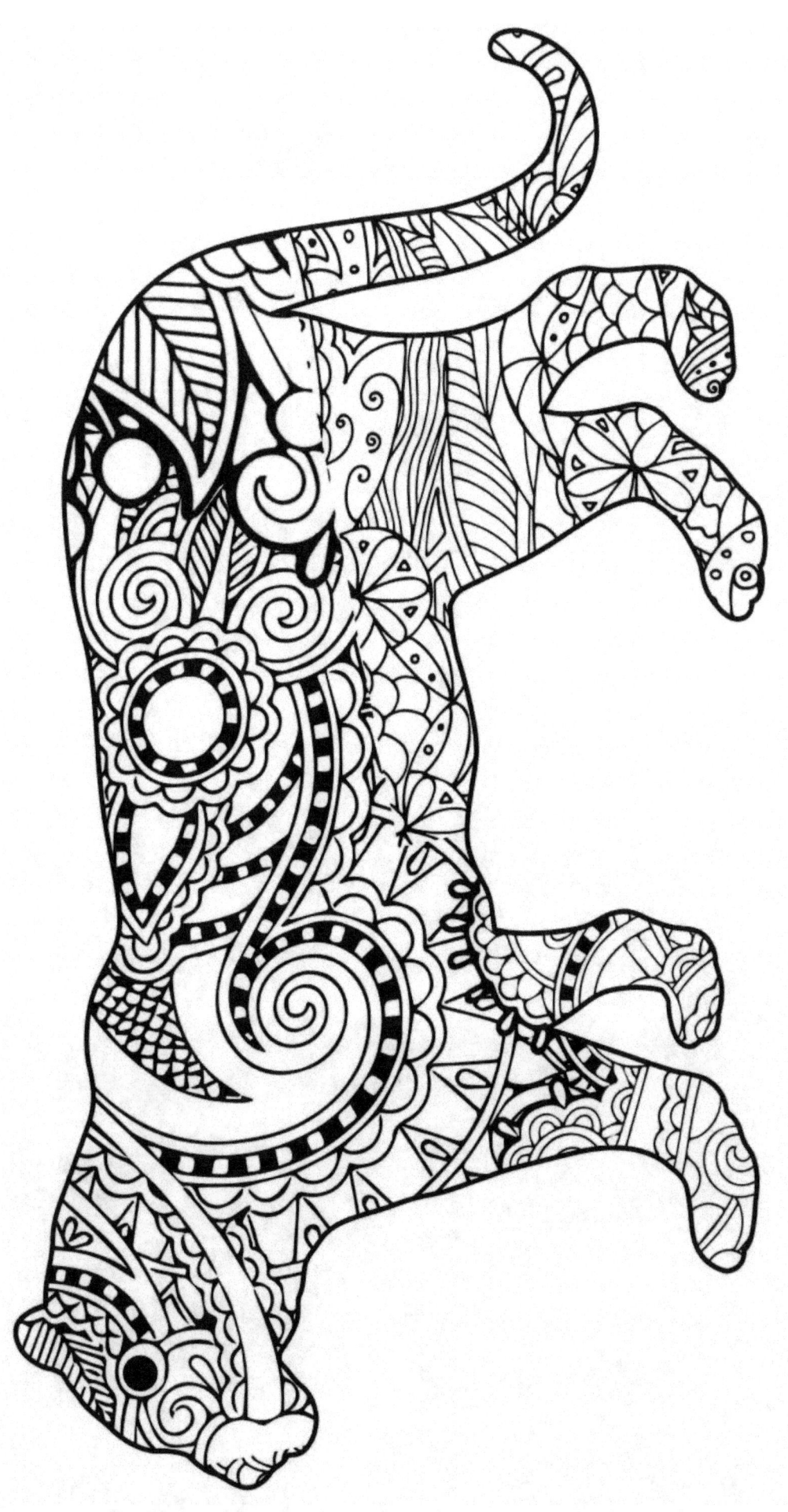

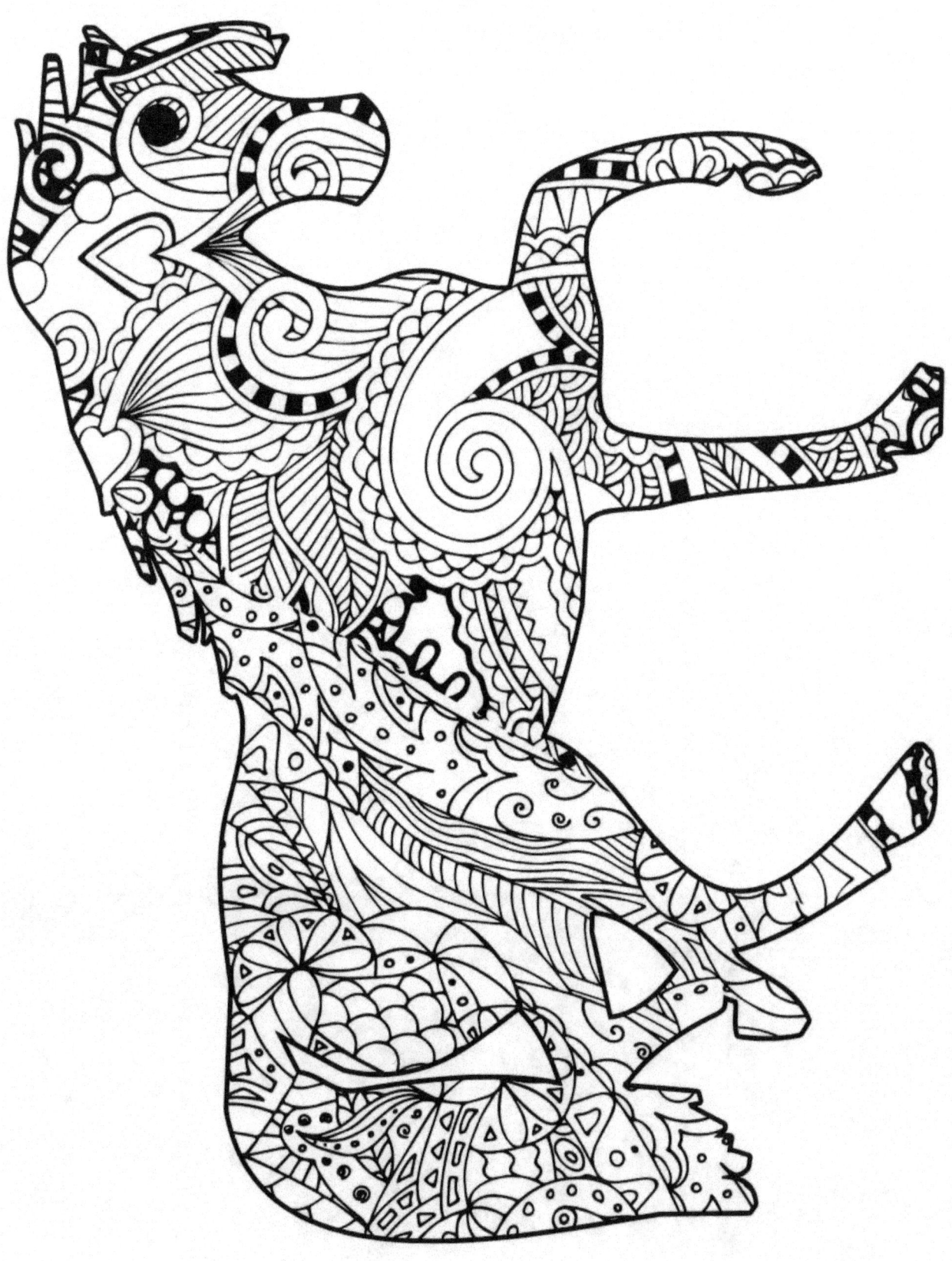

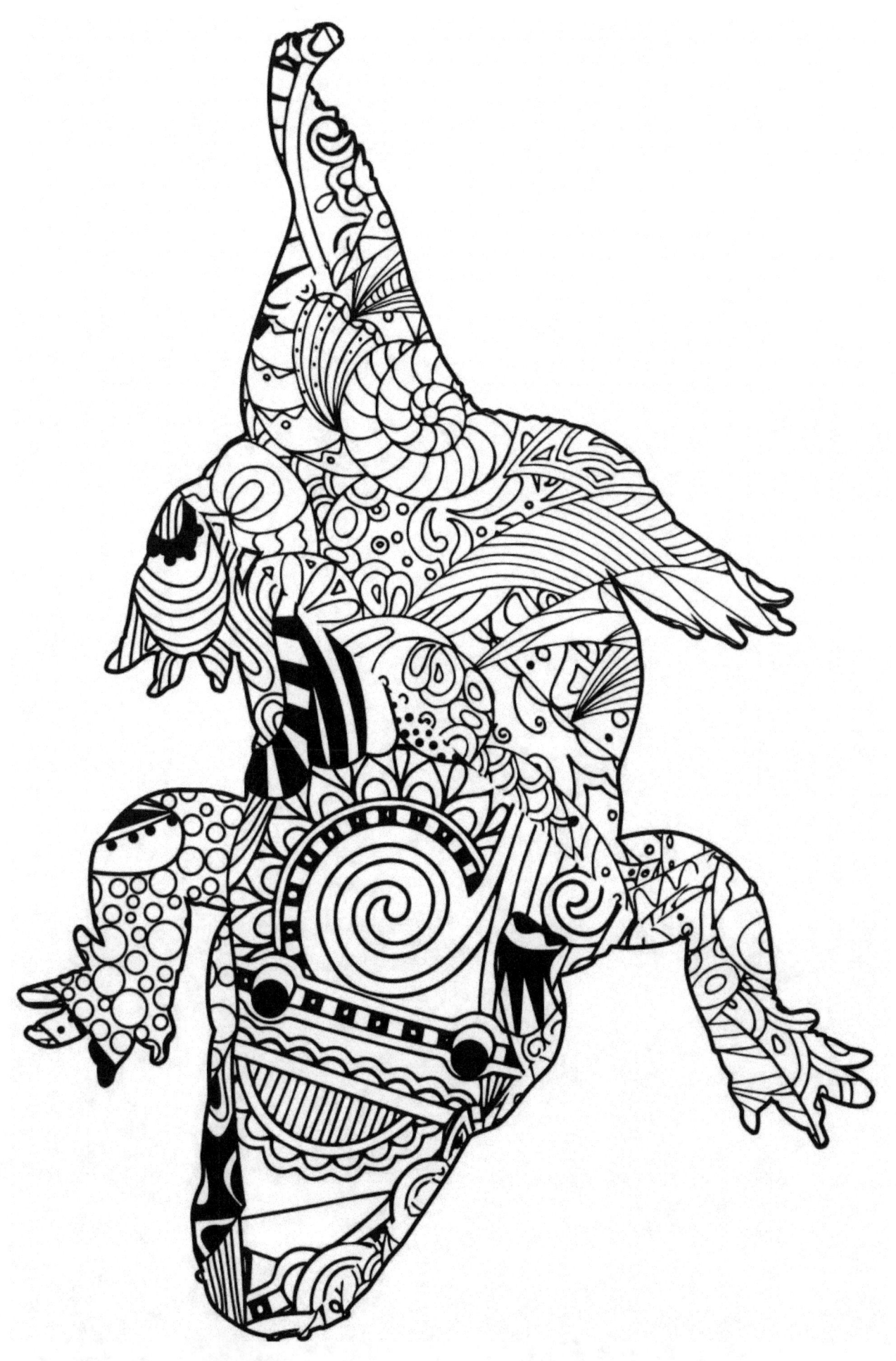

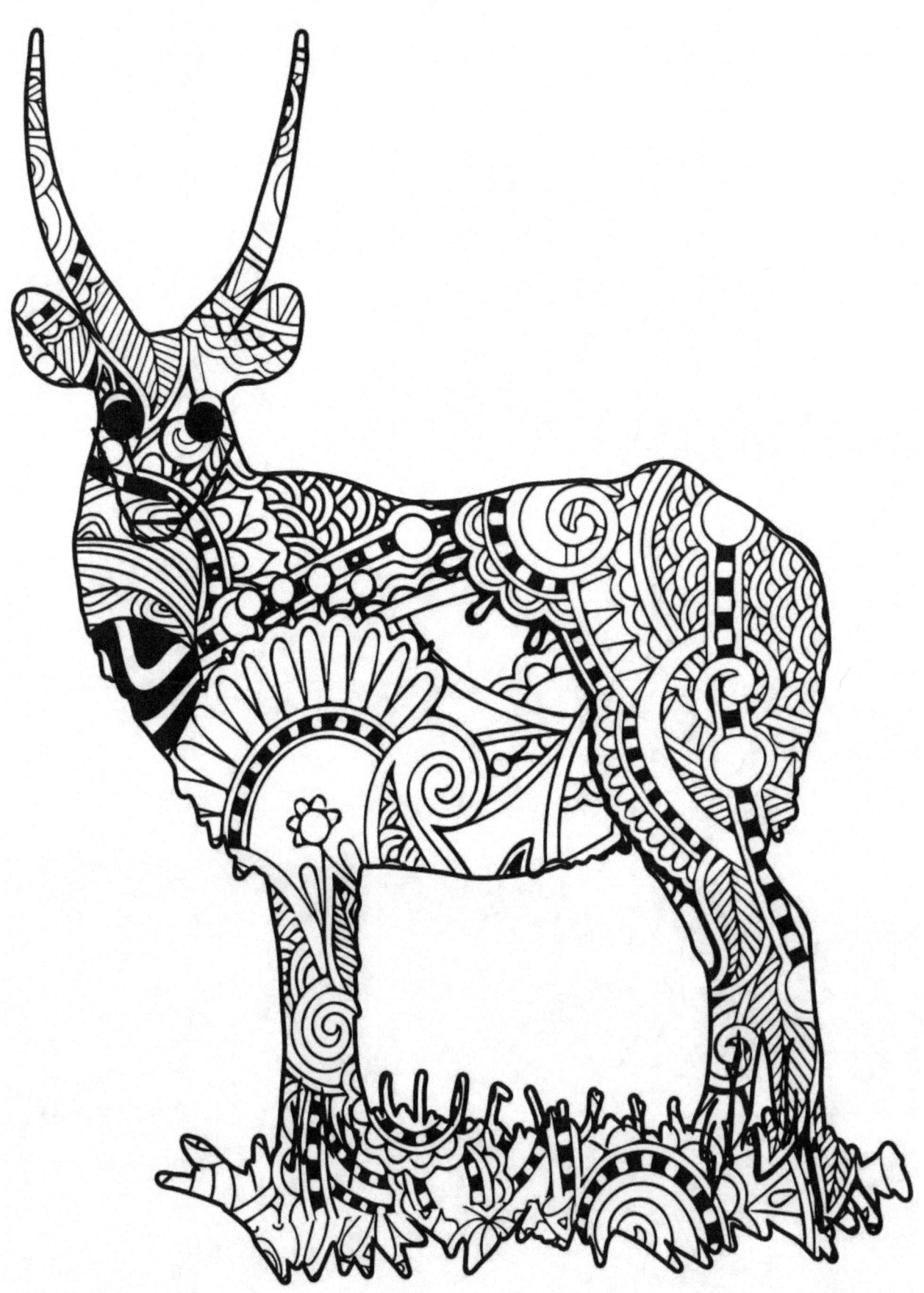

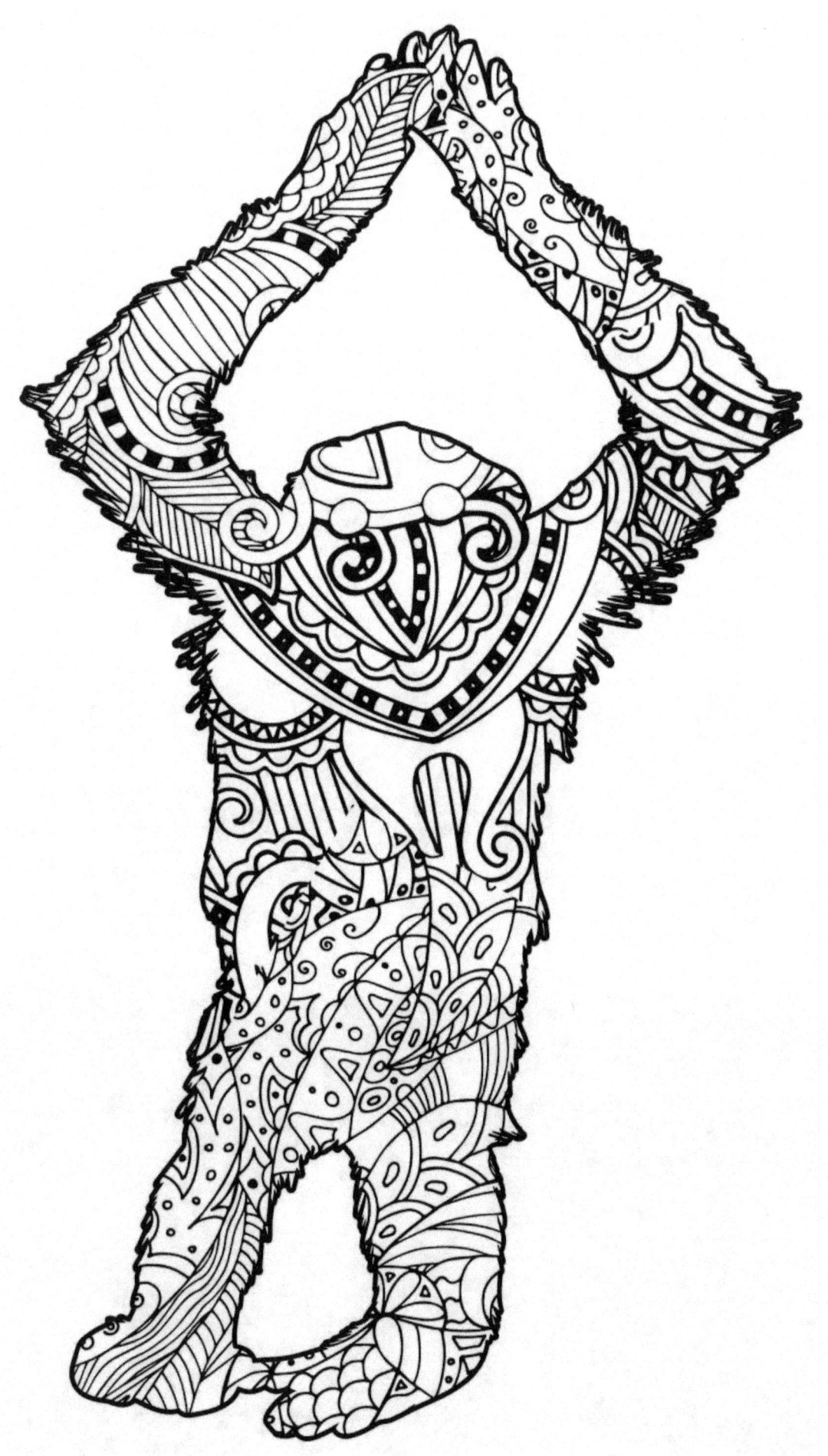

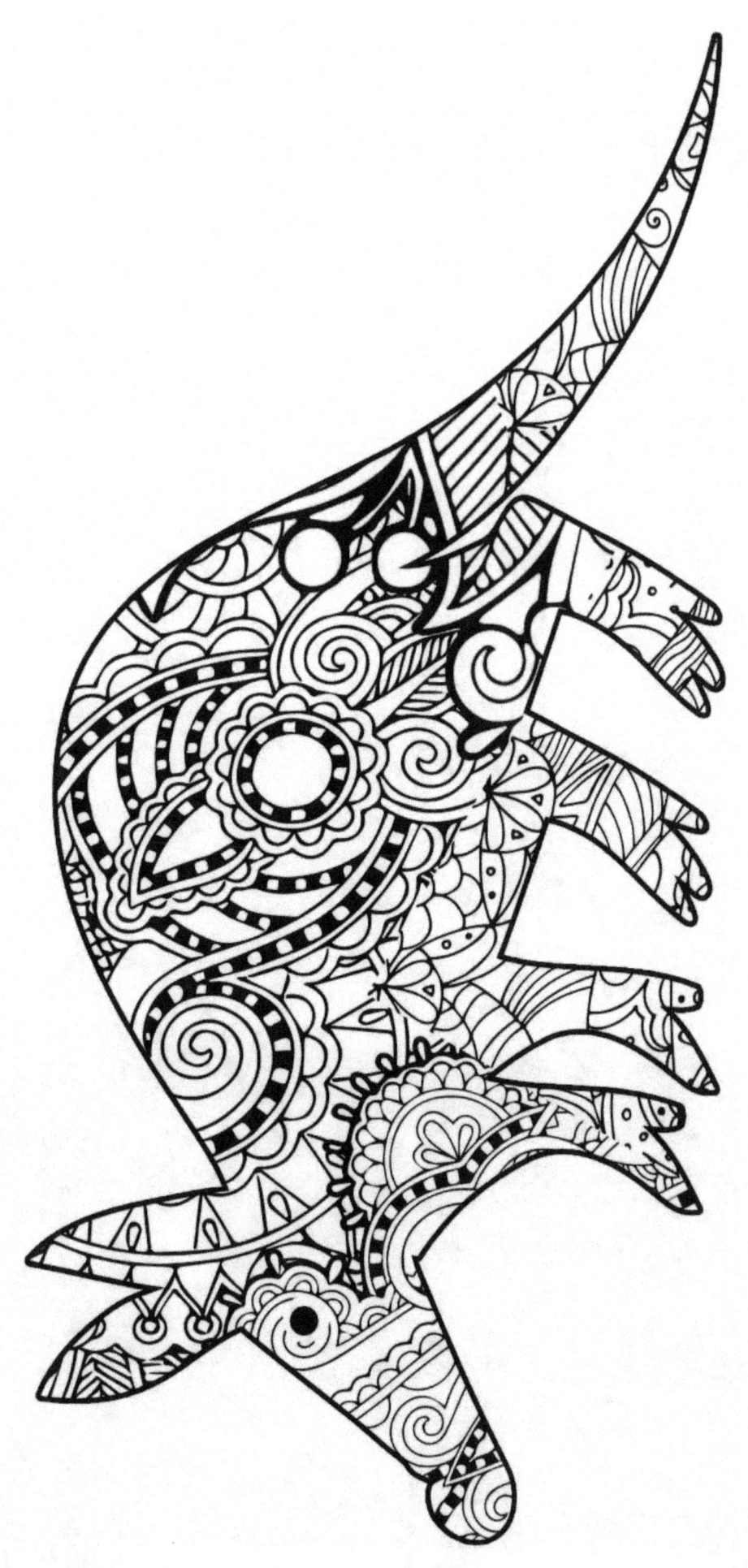

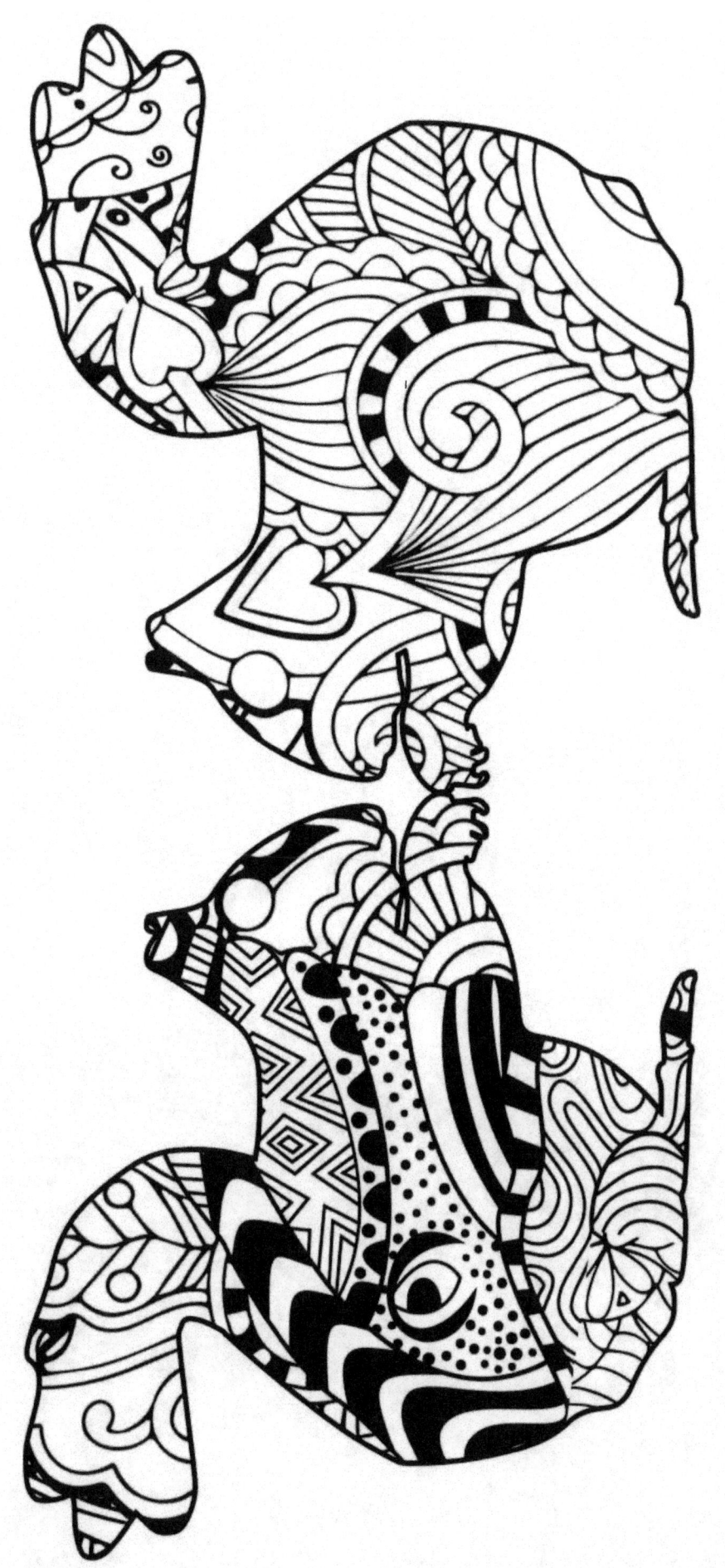

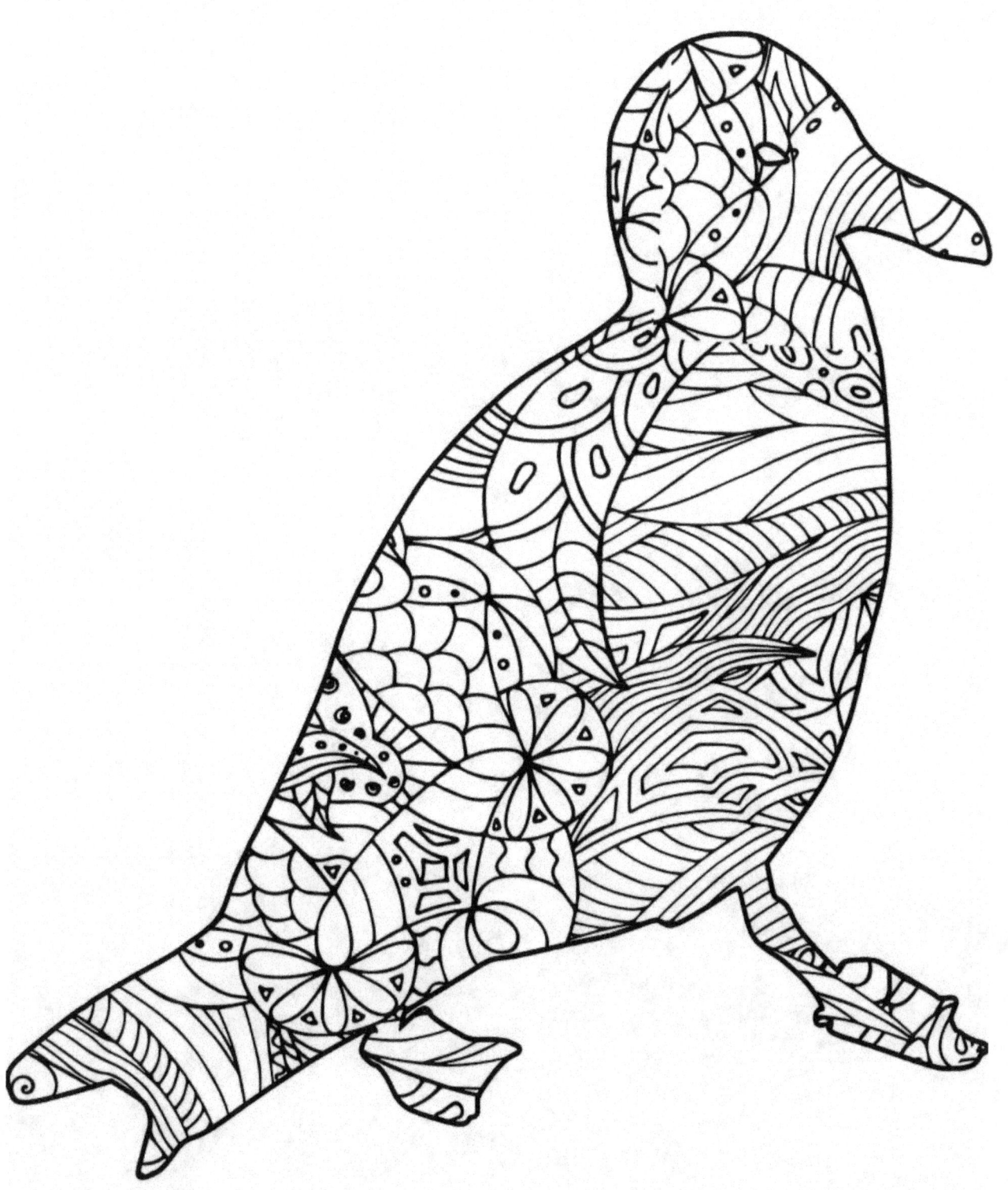

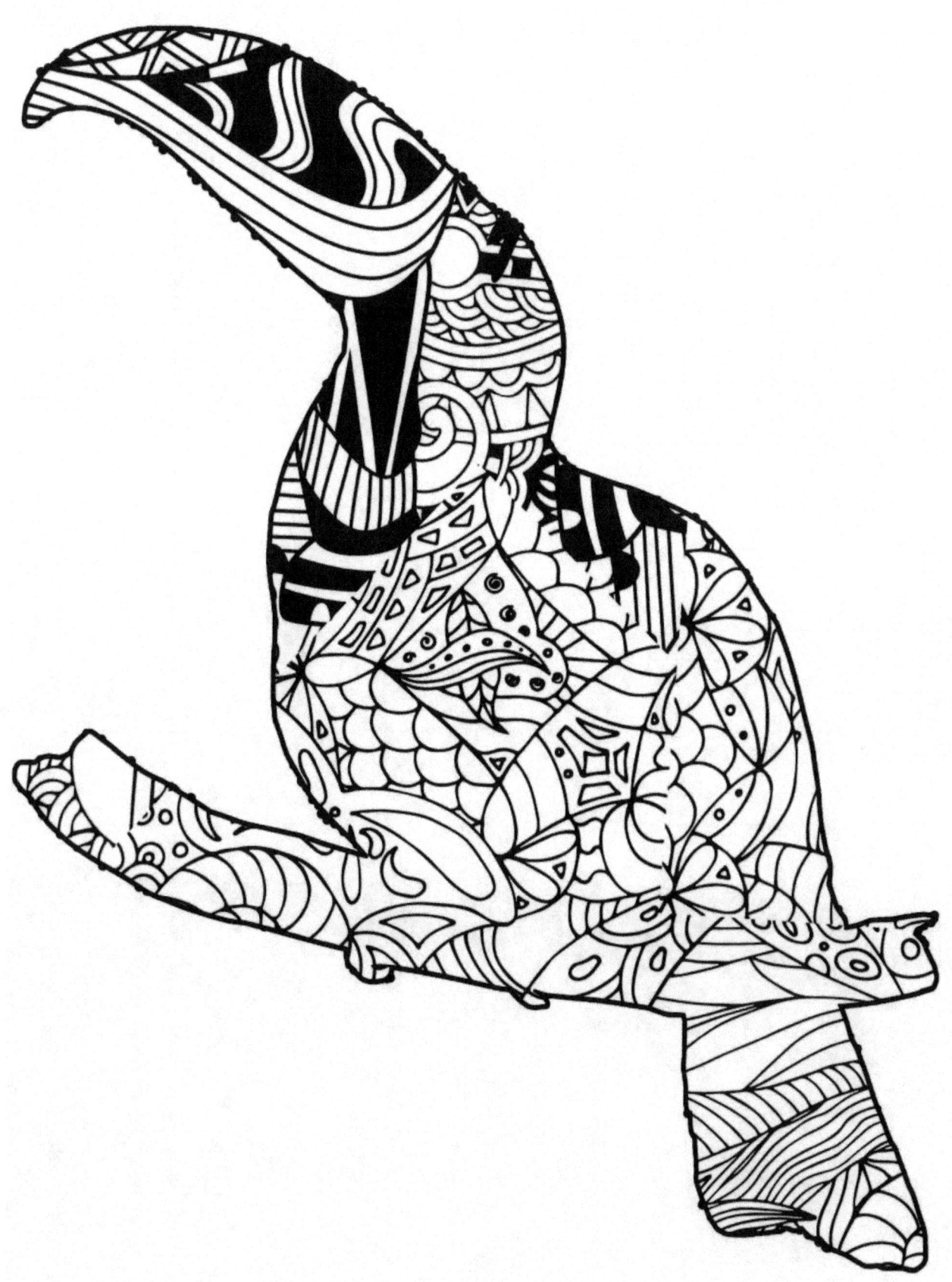

www.ingramcontent.com/pod-product-compliance
Lightning Source LLC
Chambersburg PA
CBHW080824180526
45168CB00006B/2567

* 9 7 8 1 5 1 6 9 6 9 7 9 1 *